Access to History

General Editor: Keith Randell

War and Peace: International Relations 1914-1945

David Williamson

Hodder & Stoughton

A MEMBER OF THE HODDER HEADLINE GROUP

The cover illustration is *The Trail of War,* 1919 (depicting destroyed Turkish airlines) by Sydney Carline (1888-1929), courtesy of York City Art Gallery/Bridgeman Art Library, London.

Some other titles in the series:

Rivalry and Accord: International Relations 1870-1914 John Lowe	ISBN 0 340 51806 5
Britain: Foreign and Imperial Affairs 1919-39 Alan Farmer	ISBN 0 340 55928 4
Britain: Foreign and Imperial Affairs 1939-64 Alan Farmer	ISBN 0 340 59256 7
Italy: Liberalism and Fascism 1870-1945 Mark Robson	ISBN 0 340 54548 8
Stalin and Khrushchev: The USSR 1924-64 Michael Lynch	ISBN 0 340 53335 8
Germany: The Third Reich 1933-45 Geoff Layton	ISBN 0 340 53847 3

British Library Cataloguing in Publication Data

A catalogue for this book is
available from the British Library

ISBN 0-340-57165-9

First published 1994

Impression number 10 9 8 7 6 5 4 3 2
Year 1998 1997 1996 1995

Typeset by Sempringham publishing, Bedford
Printed in Great Britain for Hodder & Stoughton Educational,
a division of Hodder Headline Plc, 338 Euston Road, London NW1 3BH
by Redwood Books, Trowbridge, Wilts

Contents

Preface

To the general reader

Although the *Access to History* series has been designed with the needs of students studying the subject at higher examination levels very much in mind, it also has a great deal to offer the general reader. The main body of the text (i.e. ignoring the Study Guides at the ends of chapters) forms a readable and yet stimulating survey of a coherent topic as studied by historians. However, each author's aim has not merely been to provide a clear explanation of what happened in the past (to interest and inform): it has also been assumed that most readers wish to be stimulated into thinking further about the topic and to form opinions of their own about the significance of the events that are described and discussed (to be challenged). Thus, although no prior knowledge of the topic is expected on the reader's part, she or he is treated as an intelligent and thinking person throughout. The author tends to share ideas and possibilities with the reader, rather than passing on numbers of so-called 'historical truths'.

To the student reader

There are many ways in which the series can be used by students studying History at a higher level. It will, therefore, be worthwhile thinking about your own study strategy before you start your work on this book. Obviously, your strategy will vary depending on the aim you have in mind, and the time for study that is available to you.

If, for example, you want to acquire a general overview of the topic in the shortest possible time, the following approach will probably be the most effective:

1 Read chapter 1 and think about its contents.
2 Read the 'Making notes' section at the end of chapter 2 and decide whether it is necessary for you to read this chapter.
3 If it is, read the chapter, stopping at each heading to note down the main points that have been made.
4 Repeat stage 2 (and stage 3 where appropriate) for all the other chapters.

If, however, your aim is to gain a thorough grasp of the topic, taking however much time is necessary to do so, you may benefit from carrying out the same procedure with each chapter, as follows:

1 Read the chapter as fast as you can, and preferably at one sitting.
2 Study the flow diagram at the end of the chapter, ensuring that you understand the general 'shape' of what you have just read.

3 Read the 'Making notes' section (and the 'Answering essay questions' section, if there is one) and decide what further work you need to do on the chapter. In particularly important sections of the book, this will involve reading the chapter a second time and stopping at each heading to think about (and to write a summary of) what you have just read.
4 Attempt the 'Source-based questions' section. It will sometimes be sufficient to think through your answers, but additional understanding will often be gained by forcing yourself to write them down.

When you have finished the main chapters of the book, study the 'Further Reading' section and decide what additional reading (if any) you will do on the topic.

This book has been designed to help make your studies both enjoyable and successful. If you can think of ways in which this could have been done more effectively, please write to tell me. In the meantime, I hope that you will gain greatly from your study of History.

Keith Randell

Acknowledgements

The Publishers would like to thank the following for permission to reproduce illustrations in this volume:

Cover - *The Trail of War,* 1919 (depicting destroyed Turkish airlines) by Sydney Carline (1888-1929), courtesy of York City Art Gallery/ Bridgeman Art Library, London. Punch Publications pages 19, 37 and 60; Centre for the Study of Cartoon and Caricature, University of Kent at Canterbury / Solo Syndication, London p. 98; Washington Post p. 120; Editors Press Service, Inc., copyright © 1945 The Chicago Tribune p. 138.

CHAPTER 1

Introduction

1 The Era of the World Wars, 1914-45: Problems of Interpretation

It is always a temptation for historians to divide past events into neat eras or epochs. The period 1914-45 seems to fit easily into such a pattern. It started with a major war apparently fought to prevent German domination of Europe and it ended with a second and more bloody war waged for the same purpose. In short, the years 1914-39 seem to form a clearly identifiable 'era of the German wars'. Churchill and many of his contemporaries, thinking of the great struggle in central Europe which raged between 1618 and 1648, characterised this period as a new Thirty Years War. At first glance this description seems appropriate. After all, Germany was not destroyed in 1918 and the peace settlements of 1919-20 appeared to many people at the time to be just a temporary truce before a new war broke out. Marshal Foch, the Commander-in-Chief of the Allied armies in 1918, summed up the Treaty of Versailles as 'an armistice for twenty years'. Between 1919 and 1923 France went to the very edge of war in an attempt to enforce Versailles and ten years later with Hitler's seizure of power the count down to the Second World War seemed to have begun.

However is it accurate to describe the whole period as 'the German wars'? Does it not in P.M.H. Bell's words 'squeeze out of our history the men and events between the wars, as though they were nothing more than ghostly inhabitants of an extended half-time interval'? There are, as you will see when you read through this book, many similarities between the German war aims in both wars, but this does not necessarily mean that the two wars were really the same conflict, although some historians like Fritz Fischer would imply that they were. After reading chapter 4 you may want to argue that between 1924 and 1930 American and European statesmen did manage to establish an international equilibrium and were well on the way to solving the German problem peacefully, and that consequently the Second World War was far from inevitable. Perhaps it was the economic depression of 1929-33, and not the unfinished business of 1918, which by bringing Hitler to power caused the Second World War?

So far we have only discussed 'the German wars', but you will quickly discover that although these were indeed epic struggles, there were other conflicts in eastern Europe and Russia, 1918-21, North Africa and the Mediterranean, 1935-40, and the Far East from 1931 onwards that all helped collectively to destabilise the peace settlements and weaken Europe. However much historians may debate about the causes of the two world wars, all agree on the irreparable damage they did to Europe's prosperity and position in the world.

2 The Great Powers in 1914

In the early years of the twentieth century the developed world seemed to be moving in contradictory directions. On one hand it was becoming economically more inter-dependent, but politically the Great Powers continued to insist upon their absolute independence. In the words of Professor Northedge, they surveyed 'each other through their visors like medieval knights in the jousting field'.

a) Germany

By 1914 Germany was sufficiently strong both economically and militarily to threaten Europe, but not powerful enough to dominate it effortlessly. The new German Empire was therefore a potential challenge to the rest of Europe, which could easily be provoked by clumsy or aggressive German policies into forming an anti-German coalition. Bismarck realised this only too well and initially, after his great victory over France, which enabled German unification to take place, he went out of his way to stress that Germany desired no further territorial changes. He skilfully managed to isolate France and establish a diplomatic system centred on Berlin. He negotiated the Triple Alliance with Austria-Hungary and Italy and a limited non-aggression pact with Russia, but his system broke down after his dismissal in 1890. The new German Chancellor did not renew the agreement with Russia on the grounds that it was more advantageous to Russia than to Germany. Not surprisingly, in 1894 France rapidly seized the chance to escape isolation by negotiating a defensive treaty with Russia. In 1898 Germany made a further miscalculation when she embarked upon a massive naval construction programme, which she hoped would ultimately force Britain to tolerate the emergence of Germany as a major colonial Power and join the Triple Alliance. However, it had the opposite effect and drove Britain into co-operating more closely with France and Russia.

The Bismarckian web of alliances was replaced by an unstable system composed of two opposing groups, led by Germany and France respectively, neither of which was strong enough to dominate Europe or create a real balance of power. Outside Europe, Germany, despite the fact that she had investments and trading interests all over the world, found herself excluded by Britain and France from participating in the control of the economically most valuable areas of Asia and Africa. After 1885, when Bismarck created a modest colonial empire in Africa and the Far East, Germany was unable to add appreciably to her possessions. Consequently it is not altogether unsurprising that important interest groups inside Germany began to advocate the policy of *Mitteleuropa* or German economic and political domination of central and eastern Europe. In that sense there was, as Fritz Fischer has stressed, a certain continuity in German foreign policy between the kaiser's regime and the Third Reich.

b) Austria-Hungary and the Ottoman Empire

Germany's only reliable ally on the eve of war in 1914 was the Austro-Hungarian Empire. In effect the Empire was two virtually independent states which shared a common crown and operated a joint foreign policy. The Hungarians strengthened the anti-Russian tendency of Austrian foreign policy as they feared the impact of Russia's sympathy for the Balkan Slavs on their own large Slav population. Austria-Hungary contained within its frontiers some 11 different nationalities which were to face the peace-makers of 1919 with insuperable problems when they came to draw up the frontiers of the new small states that replaced the Empire. Austria's fate was perceived by contemporaries to be linked with the Ottoman Empire. Vienna feared that the same Balkan

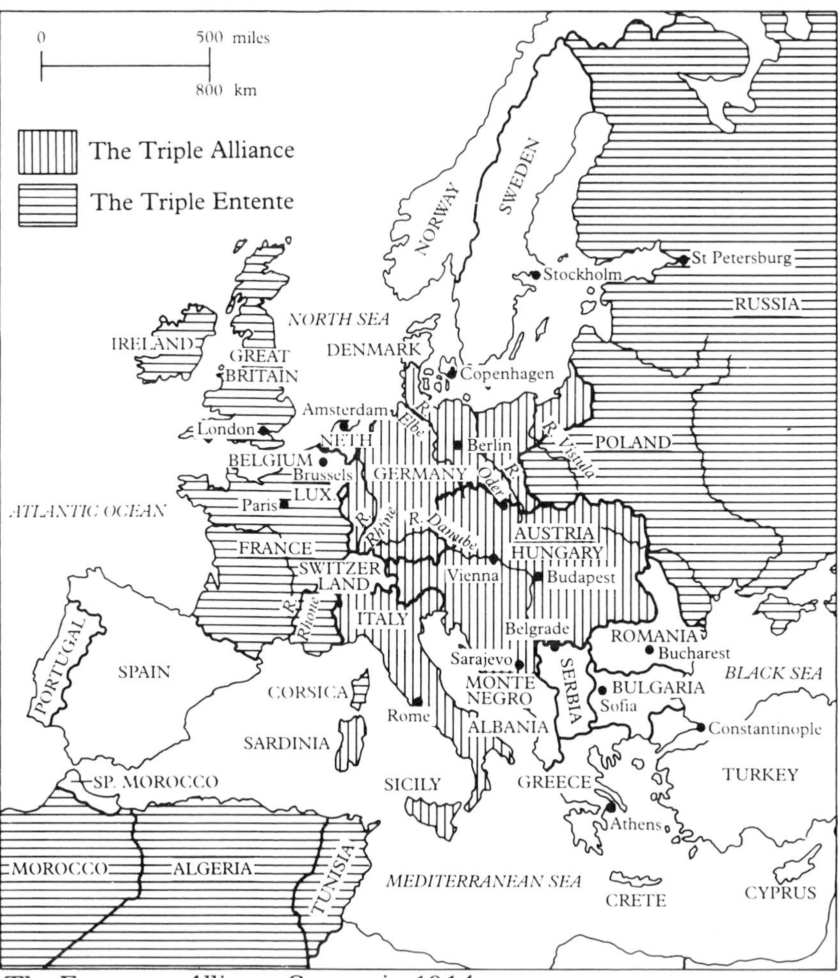

The European Alliance System in 1914

nationalism which had virtually driven the Turks out of the Balkans by 1912 would eventually also destroy the Habsburg Empire. Above all the Empire felt itself threatened by the emergence of a strong independent Serbia, which it was convinced enjoyed the backing of Russia and was aiming to liberate the Serbs in the Austrian province of Bosnia. The Empire's main defence against Russia remained the Austro-German alliance of 1879. Through this alliance the German problem became linked with the Balkan or eastern question with potentially lethal consequences for the peace of Europe, as Berlin's support for Austria began to be regarded by France and Russia as a camouflage for German expansion into south-eastern Europe.

An eminent German general was to describe his country's two principal wartime allies, the Ottoman Empire and Austria-Hungary as 'rotting corpses'. If the Austrian Empire was a 'corpse', it only became one in December 1918 after four years of total war. In the nineteenth century it had played a vital role in stabilising south-eastern Europe and its disintegration made it easier later for first Nazi Germany and then Soviet Russia to dominate the whole region.

The Ottoman Empire was certainly in a more advanced stage of decay than Austria, but even before 1914 there were hints of the remarkable revival of energy that was to galvanise the Turks into forcing the Allies in 1922-3 to renegotiate the punitive peace Treaty of Sèvres (see pages 41-3). In 1908 the Young Turk movement, in a desperate attempt to prevent the disintegration of the Ottoman Empire, seized power and begun the process of modernising Turkey. Turkey was to be drawn increasingly into the German orbit. In 1913 the German government was invited to send a military mission to Constantinople to help modernise and re-equip the Turkish army.

c) Italy: Germany's Ally?

Italy had been unified in the same decade as Germany, and liked to see herself as a Great Power in the traditions of Ancient Rome. In reality she was one of the weakest of the European Powers both economically and militarily. In 1896 her attempt to annex Abyssinia ended with her humiliating defeat at Adowa.

In 1882 she allied herself through the Triple Alliance with Germany and her old enemy Austria. She hoped that a further French defeat by Germany might win her a share in France's North African empire. She did, however, remain open to offers from other Powers and it was not a difficult task for the French to neutralise her by agreeing in 1900 to recognise the Turkish province of Tripoli as a potential Italian sphere of interest. Thus when Italy renewed the Triple Alliance in 1902, she specifically stipulated that she could not join in a war against France.

d) The Franco-Russian Alliance

In 1914 France was arguably already a second-class Power. She had been defeated by Prussia in 1871 and both economically and demographically she had been overtaken by Germany and Britain. Her industrial base was small and her coal deposits a fraction of Britain's and Germany's. She had nevertheless managed to rebuild and re-equip her army and to a certain extent compensate for the relative smallness of her population by building up a large North African empire, which was to be crucial in providing men in time of war. However the key to her survival as an independent power lay in her ability to forge a strong alliance system to contain Germany. The crucial move in this direction was the alliance with Russia in 1894.

Although Russia had a population that was double Germany's and an economy that was developing fast by 1914, the effective deployment of her potentially overwhelming strength was always threatened by domestic instability, which had already boiled over into open revolt in 1905. By 1914 foreign observers were unanimous that Russia was sitting on 'the edge of a volcano'.

Given these worrying doubts about the ultimate effectiveness of the Russian alliance, the French tried to underpin it by bringing years of Anglo-French friction and rivalry to an end through the negotiation of the 1904 colonial agreement with London. Germany's isolation in Europe by 1914 is striking evidence of the success of French policy in breaking out of the strait jacket in which Bismarck had initially so successfully confined her.

e) Great Britain: France's 'Unofficial Ally'

A Chinese statesman had observed to Lord Salisbury in the 1890s that Britain and China 'were two empires on the decline'. Although Britain was enormously wealthy in 1914, the fundamental basis of her power was being eroded. She had built up her wealth on the basis of her domination of the world's trade underpinned by her control of the seas. By 1900 this had been dangerously weakened. France, Russia, Germany and even Italy were all capable of playing a global role and moving into areas such as China, where previously Britain had enjoyed a virtual trade monopoly. Economically Britain was being overtaken by Germany and the United States and her absolute control of the seas was threatened by the construction of the German fleet. Through its sheer size the British Empire became an unwieldy and vulnerable giant. As a world trading and financial power Britain's main priority was peace. She was thus unwilling to enter a Continental alliance that might lead to war. In 1902 she secured her position against a possible attack from a combination of Powers in the Far East by a defensive alliance with Japan. Otherwise she attempted to defuse challenges to her position by a policy of compromise and appeasement, which enabled her successfully to negotiate the Anglo-French and Anglo-Russian colonial agreements of 1904 and 1907. She was ready to appease Germany, too, but only at the cost of Germany abandoning its naval challenge. In many ways Germany was right to see Britain as a formidable barrier to its expansion. Essentially Britain as a world trading power could not tolerate a German victory in Europe as this would then lead to the global domination of Germany, which would in effect turn the British Empire into a German satellite. To all intents and purposes Britain was therefore an ally of France even though she had signed no binding agreement with her.

f) The Flanking Powers: Japan and the United States of America

By 1914 the world-wide expansion of the European Powers had created a new global balance in which both Japan and America were becoming increasingly involved. Over the next 30 years both Powers were to play a crucial role in international developments. Japan was already beginning to exploit European rivalries to strengthen her position in the Far East, while it was becoming clear that America's long, secure isolation from European power politics was being put into question by the rise of Germany.

In 1914 Japan was a formidable regional power with a population of some 46 million. She had initially in 1858 been compelled to grant the western nations considerable economic privileges and rights when she opened her ports to trade with the West, but thanks to a policy of rapid modernisation she had managed to avoid becoming dependent on any one European Power. By 1899 she had not only regained her economic freedom but also embarked upon a period of territorial expansion that was only to end in 1945.

Lacking the strength to operate in isolation and foreseeing confrontation with Russia in Manchuria, she negotiated an alliance with Britain, which enabled her to defeat Russia in 1905 and strengthen her position in Korea and southern Manchuria. Driven on by the intense nationalism of her officer corps and the various patriotic societies, both of which were to exercise a powerful influence on her foreign policy up to 1945, the Japanese government attempted to exploit the mounting chaos in China caused by the overthrow in 1912 of the Chinese Imperial government by internal revolution. For the next 30 years the main aim of Japanese foreign policy was directed towards exploiting the ever deepening chaos in China in order to build up its own economically self-sufficient empire.

The United States of America for most of the nineteenth century had been shielded from any danger of Continental European intervention by

Britain's undisputed supremacy of the seas. America had consequently been able to enjoy the benefits of neutrality and isolation in complete security. However, the formidable challenge to the Royal Navy launched by Germany did open up the disturbing prospect of a German naval presence in the Atlantic and by 1914 the United States had taken the precaution of building up the third largest navy in the world. Like Japan, America also became an imperial power. In the colonial war against Spain in 1898 American forces had seized Cuba and Puerto Rico in the Caribbean and the Philippines and Hawaii in the Far East. Although American public opinion was still isolationist, America's extensive financial and economic interests in both Europe and the Far East made it increasingly more difficult for her to keep out of world affairs.

Making notes on 'Introduction'

This is an introductory chapter aiming to put across to you three main themes. Firstly it indicates some of the problems involved in studying the years 1914-45. Secondly it briefly looks at the individual foreign policies of the Great Powers during the period 1890-1914 and shows how these policies were influenced by the domestic political and economic situation within each state. Try to identify the various strengths and weaknesses (political, economic, military, strategic, etc...) of the Powers and their foreign policy aims. Ask yourself to what extent these aims grew out of the domestic, economic and military situations in which the Powers found themselves. In what way does this chapter help you to answer the following questions: What were the main areas of tension in the world by 1914 and what were the underlying causes of these? To what extent was Germany isolated by 1914? As this book is primarily concerned with international affairs after 1914, your notes on this chapter should be brief. For further details about the pre-1914 international situation look at John Lowe, *Rivalry and Accord: International Relations, 1870-1914* in the *Access to History* series. Remember that there is no virtue in writing out page after page of factual information. Notes need to be precise and aimed at answering or explaining key questions about the period you are studying.

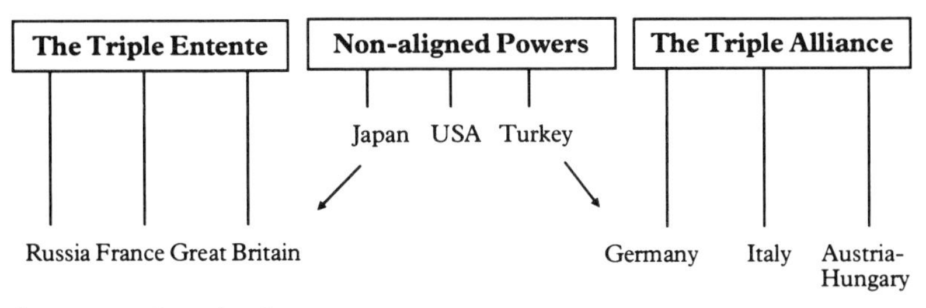

Summary - Introduction

CHAPTER 2

The International Politics of the First World War

1 From Balkan War to European War

In 1914, as was seen in the last chapter, the European Powers were confronted with a series of problems any one of which had the potential for causing war. The assassination of the Austrian Crown Prince, Archduke Franz Ferdinand, on 28 June 1914 at Sarajevo, by a Bosnian student armed with weapons supplied by a Serbian nationalist movement, the Black Hand, triggered a rapidly escalating international crisis. Each Great Power felt at the crucial moment that its vital interests were involved and that in its defence war was an acceptable policy. Vienna seized on the opportunity provided by the assassination to gain German support for what it hoped would be a short sharp war against Serbia, which would effectively weaken her and stop her support for the Bosnian Serbs. The German Chancellor agreed with the Austrian analysis of the Serbian threat, behind which he also saw Russia's influence and urged the Austrians to take 'immediate action'. The Germans hoped at this stage for a successful but localised Balkan war which would lead to the strengthening of both their own and Austria's diplomatic position in Europe. However, this plan started to go wildly wrong when after the Austrian declaration of war on Serbia on 28 July, the Russians began to mobilise. In the Balkan crises of 1909 and 1913 they had failed to back the Serbs, but this time the Tsar was advised that an Austrian victory over Serbia would seriously damage Russia's credibility and open the way to a dramatic increase in Austrian and German influence in the Balkans. Serbia's preservation was also vital as she would be the nucleus of any future alliance system devised by the Russians to contain Austria and Germany in the Balkans.

A.J.P. Taylor has argued that the outbreak of the First World War was 'caused almost entirely by the rival plans for mobilisation'. This was certainly so in a technical sense once Russia began to mobilise, as the German war plan (the Schlieffen Plan) had been drawn up on the assumption that Russia's ally, France, would have to be defeated in the weeks before Russia could fully deploy her troops. Thus when the Russians ignored an ultimatum to suspend their mobilisation, the Germans declared war on Russia on 1 August. The Balkan war had now become a Continental war. The Germans attempted to keep the French out of the war by demanding a declaration of neutrality, but when this was rejected on the grounds that France needed to preserve the freedom to 'act in accordance with her interests', Germany declared war and began to implement the Schlieffen Plan by invading Belgium. Would a more subtle approach by the Germans have kept the French out of the war? This seems unlikely as the French government had no intention of standing back and watching the destruction of Russia, who was their only major ally on the Continent. Ironically the German declaration of war merely made it easier for the French government to unite public opinion behind the war effort. The German invasion of Belgium (a necessary part of the Schlieffen Plan) was to have a similar impact on British public opinion as it enabled the war party within the Cabinet to win over their colleagues and Parliament to support British intervention on 4 August after the Germans had rejected the British ultimatum to evacuate Belgium. In reality Britain had little choice but to back France if she were to avoid a German-dominated Europe. Also, like the other Powers who were to enter the war later, Britain needed to ensure that she would have a powerful voice at the peace conference after the war was over in order to preserve her own influence in the world.

2 The Widening Conflict

From the militarily point of view the First World War was not a truly global conflict, as most of the fighting took place in Europe and the Middle East. Nevertheless by 1917 there was hardly a country in the world which was not involved in some way in the struggle. The war was both a threat and an opportunity to many neutral Powers. On the one hand their very neutrality could make them vulnerable as their interests might well be ignored by the victors at the end of the war. Portugal, for instance, was anxious to fight on the side of the Entente in order to prevent her colonies from becoming a potential bargaining counter between Britain and Germany. Even President Wilson of the United States came to the conclusion that only by entering the war would he be able to use American power decisively to shape the post-war world. However, on the other hand, the frantic search for allies by the belligerents, especially when it became obvious by the autumn of 1914 that there would be no quick victory, tempted many of the neutral powers to sell their support to the highest bidder. The first two Powers to exploit the opportunities presented to them by the war were Japan and the Ottoman Empire. In both states it was nationalist politicians who seized the initiative and forced their governments into war.

a) Japan Seizes her Chance, August 1914

For Japan the war presented immense opportunities to increase her power in China and the Pacific region at a time when the energies of the European Powers were absorbed in Europe. The Japanese responded enthusiastically on 23 August to a British request to declare war on Germany. The British had originally intended that the Japanese navy should merely help with convoy duties in the Pacific, but the Japanese refused to be relegated to a minor role and much to the alarm of Britain, Australia and the United States, proceeded to seize German territory in the Chinese province of Shantung as well as the German Pacific islands. In January 1915 the Japanese pushed their luck further and presented China with the Twenty-one Demands, which not only included the recognition of the Japanese claims to Shantung and southern Manchuria (see map on page 83) but also proposed that the Chinese government should appoint Japanese advisers. This last demand would have turned China into a Japanese protectorate and was only dropped after strong British and American objections. However, the rest of the demands were accepted by China in May 1915.

b) The Ottoman Empire Follows Suite, October 1914

The choices facing Turkey in 1914 were more complex than those confronting Japan. Unlike Japan, the Ottoman Empire was not a vigorous and disciplined power operating in an area which the Western Powers found increasingly difficult to control. Even a German victory would have made little difference to Japan's position in the Pacific. Ottoman Turkey was a fragile, declining empire, highly vulnerable to pressure from the Great Powers. She could certainly not afford to back the losing side, but remaining neutral had its dangers too, especially if Russia emerged greatly strengthened from the war. Thus initially there was pressure within the government to back Germany on the assumption that the defeat of Russia could lessen the pressure on Turkey's northern frontiers. Yet once Britain entered the war the Ottoman government, aware of its vulnerability, had second thoughts. Nevertheless both the Germans and the Allies attempted to secure, if not Turkish support, at least her neutrality by rival offers of concessions. In the end the Germans were able to outbid their enemies by promising their support for the Turkish annexation of Russian border territory and possibly the restoration of the Aegean islands ceded to Greece. London seriously damaged its bargaining position by refusing to hand over two Turkish warships which had just been constructed in Britain, while the Germans were able to strengthen their influence on Constantinople by despatching a couple of cruisers to the Dardanelles. On 29 October Turkey entered the war on the German side. Turkey was to prove a serious threat to Britain's Imperial communications through the Suez Canal and to force her to employ large-scale forces in its defence.

c) Italy Exerts her Bargaining Power, August 1914-May 1915

Once Britain declared war, Italy with her vulnerable coastline had no alternative but to opt out of the Triple Alliance and declare her neutrality. This decision was reinforced by her reluctance to see a victorious Austria-Hungary strengthening her position in the Adriatic. Ideally the Italian government, uncomfortably aware of its military weakness, wanted to enter the war at a point when the Allies had already virtually defeated the Central powers, but realistically it also realised that its ability to wring concessions from the Allies would be at its most effective while Germany and Austria-Hungary were still undefeated. Although negotiating with the Allies, it also remained open to offers from the Central Powers. In December 1914 Prince von Bülow, the former German Chancellor, was sent on a special mission to Rome. He reported that the Italian Foreign minister, Baron Sonnino,

> 1 made no bones about giving me his views of the position ... As war objectives the Allies had promised Italy all Austrian territories peopled by Italian subjects. Should Austria wish to be assured that Italy would not enter the war against her, she must ... propose
> 5 definite concessions ... [which] would ... have to be tendered in a decent and dignified fashion. ... the indispensable minimum was immediate ... cession of the Italian Tyrol; the Trentino; a promise of the autonomy of Trieste within ... the Dual Monarchy and better treatment for the Italians in Istria and Dalmatia.

In dealing with Italy Germany was handicapped by the fact that her alliance with Austria-Hungary prevented her from making sweeping concessions in the very areas in which Italy was most interested. To a more limited extent Britain's and France's alliance with Russia also ensured that there were limits to what they could offer Italy along the Adriatic coast line, as Russia was anxious to support Serbia's claims to Dalmatia. Nevertheless, the Allies could offer more than the Central Powers and were ultimately able to conclude an alliance with Italy. By the Treaty of London in May 1915 Italy entered the war on the Allied side and was promised not only the Austrian territories of South Tyrol, Istria and nearly half the Dalmatian coastline, but also territory in Africa and the Middle East if Germany lost her colonies and the Ottoman Empire were partitioned.

d) Bulgaria, Romania and Greece Enter the War, 1915-17

Both Bulgaria and Romania wanted territory which they hoped somehow either to win from each other or from the Turkish or Austro-Hungarian empires (see the map on page 3). Like Italy they were therefore open to bids, but, being small and weak powers, a false calculation putting them on the losing side would spell disaster for their ambitions. Consequently they attempted to remain neutral until it was clear which side was winning. To Bulgaria this point seemed to have been reached when the Russians were routed in Poland in September 1915 and Germany promised that in the event of victory she was ready to restore to Bulgarian control much of the territory lost to Greece and Romania in 1913. Romania's calculations were 'the mirror image' (Stevenson) of Bulgaria's. Primarily interested in gaining Hungarian territory, she waited until the summer of 1916 when the Allied armies appeared to be winning. Then, once she had secured promises of the future transfer of those areas in Transylvania and Bukovina (see map on page 34) where Romanians formed the majority of the population, she declared war on the Central Powers in August 1916. In Greece the decision to enter the war was not so clear cut. Opinion was polarised between those who wanted to support the Allies and those, led by the king, who wished to remain neutral. Ultimately in July 1917 Greece was forced into war by Allied pressure.

e) The American Declaration of War, 1917

In 1914 America was already a Great Power. She did not therefore need to bid for concessions from the warring rivals. Her entry into the war would almost certainly determine its outcome. It would, however, be wrong to paint a picture of American policy as being totally impartial and only coming down on the Allied side after the Germans had broken international law by deciding in January 1917 to pursue unrestricted submarine warfare against all neutral vessels trading with the Allies. The longer the war lasted the more the American economy became dependent on exporting to the Allies munitions, food and a wide range of industrial products. For instance, between 1914 and 1916 American trade with the Allies increased by 400 per cent. Unavoidably therefore American foreign policy favoured the British and French at the expense of the Central Powers. It was not only the Germans who violated international law at sea. The British did not hesitate to intercept all neutral ships trading with Germany, but President Woodrow Wilson was careful to avoid confrontation with the British. With the Germans, on the other hand, he was much tougher. When the British liner, the *Lusitania,* was sunk in May 1915 with a loss of nearly 1200 people including 124 Americans, Wilson demanded that the Germans should pay damages and cease to torpedo passenger ships. Similarly when in March 1916 the French cross-channel ferry, the Sussex, was torpedoed with heavy loss of life, Wilson again warned the Germans and categorically refused a demand from Berlin that he should also insist on British obedience to international law. The German Chancellor, Bethmann Hollweg, was reluctant to risk a rupture with the United States. Yet in January 1917, against his better judgement, he was pushed by the German High Command into sanctioning unrestricted warfare against all shipping trading with the Allies on the optimistic assumption that this would rapidly defeat Britain. Predictably, American shipping and commerce suffered, and Wilson first broke off diplomatic relations with Germany and then on 2 April declared war. American support for

Wilson's policy strengthened when British naval intelligence decoded and sent to Washington the contents of a telegram from the German Foreign Minister, Zimmermann, to the German Ambassador in Mexico suggesting that if war broke out, Mexico should be bribed by the offer of Texas to attack in the south, while Japan, too, should be encouraged to break with the Allies.

3 War Aims, 1914-17

In 1914 Russia and the Entente Powers went to war for essentially defensive reasons. Their main aim was to prevent a German dominated Europe, which would threaten their own survival as independent Great Powers. Consequently when their war aims came to be drawn up, they were primarily concerned with weakening Germany. Each ally, of course, had a different perception of the nature of the German threat. The general thrust of British policy reflected Britain's global priorities. Her war aims envisaged the destruction of German naval and colonial power, but in Europe her policy was more moderate. She insisted only on the liberation of Serbia and Belgium and was non-committal about the future status of Poland or indeed on whether Alsace-Lorraine should be returned to France. David Lloyd George, who became Prime Minister in December 1916, was also convinced that the establishment of a democratic Germany would go far to tame Prussian militarism.

France, like Britain, was slow to formulate an official war aims programme. This was largely because she was anxious to avoid prematurely raising questions that might create friction between the Allies. Only in 1916 when it seemed possible that President Wilson might try to mediate between the belligerents, did a detailed programme begin to emerge from Paris. To counter German economic domination of central Europe the French urged the continuation of close inter-allied economic co-operation after the war. They also wanted reparations, the liberation of Belgium and the restoration of Alsace-Lorraine. Although France appeared to support independence for the Czechs, in reality right up to the summer of 1918 she was anxious to preserve Austria-Hungary if only to prevent German Austria joining the Reich. As long as the Tsarist regime survived in Russia, France also regarded the question of Polish independence as essentially a domestic matter for the Tsar. French reluctance to support the Polish nationalists was further reinforced by the readiness of the Tsarist government to support French ambitions on the Rhine. By 1916 there was a consensus in French political, military and industrial circles that France's frontier must once again be the Rhine, as it had been for a short time under Napoleon. In January 1917 Briand, the French Premier, informed a senior diplomat, Paul Cambon, that:

> 1 In our eyes, Germany must no longer have a foot beyond the Rhine; the organisation of these territories, their neutrality and their temporary occupation must be considered in exchanges of opinion between the Allies. It is, however, important that France,
> 5 being the most directly concerned with the territorial status of this region, should have the casting vote in examining the solution of this serious question.

The Russians were also hoping to create a strong buffer state between themselves and Germany. In September 1914 the Tsar announced plans for a unified Poland under Russian protection. Although initially Russia did appeal to the Slav races of Austria-Hungary to rise up in revolt, in reality Russian policy did not aim at the Habsburg Empire's destruction, but was more concerned with strengthening Serbia by giving her Bosnia and as much of Dalmatia as could be preserved from Italy's claims.

Britain, France, Russia and Italy, were both allies and potential rivals who competed with each other to profit from what they hoped would be the fruits of victory. Nowhere was this more obvious than in the Middle East, which was an area of major strategic importance to both the British and French Empires. Each ally manoeuvred to lay claim to the most wealthy areas of the Turkish Empire. In March 1915 Britain and France agreed that Russia should have Constantinople and the Straits provided that their own claims on Turkish territory were satisfied. In May 1916 the British and French signed the Sykes-Picot Agreement, which after months of hard bargaining divided Mesopotamia, Syria and the Lebanon into potential spheres of influence, while Russia and Italy were later offered respectively zones in Armenia and Smyrna (see the map on page 42). The French were uncomfortably aware that Britain, as the only Power with military superiority in the area, would easily be able to revise these agreements later. Her suspicions were confirmed when in 1917 Britain decided, contrary to the Sykes-Picot Agreement, to claim the whole of Palestine. By supporting the Zionists' ambition to establish a national home for the Jews, Britain cleverly ensured America's backing for her ambitions.

In comparison with the position of her enemies Germany had more freedom to formulate her war aims as her allies were satellites rather than Powers of equal strength. Thus Germany was happy to support Austria's plans for weakening Serbia, but when it suited her to appeal to Polish nationalism by promising to set up an independent Poland, albeit one with tight economic and military links with Berlin, Austria's own plan for absorbing Russian Poland and setting up a new Polish kingdom under her own control was ruthlessly vetoed. Germany's maximum aims were formulated when she seemed to be about to win the war in September 1914. According to the 'September Programme' she wanted:

1 Security for the German Reich in west and east for all imaginable time. For this purpose France must be so weakened as to make her revival as a Great Power impossible for all time. Russia must be thrust back as far as possible from Germany's eastern frontier and
5 her domination over non-Russian vassal peoples broken.

Although Germany demanded some limited territorial concessions from France, such as the surrender of the Dunkirk-Boulogne coastline, her main intention was to control Europe indirectly through a customs union firmly dominated by herself which would include most of continental western Europe, Poland, the Scandinavian states, the Balkans, Austria-Hungary and Turkey. By creating a new Europe under German leadership she hoped to be in a position effectively to challenge Britain. Eventually she also wanted to build a large central African Empire. Although from time to time this programme was modified in details, it remained essentially the same almost until the end of the war. Indeed in April 1917 when revolution had already broken out in Russia, it was supplemented by the Kreuznach Programme which envisaged the German annexation of large areas of Poland and the Baltic provinces.

4 Peace Feelers, 1915-17

While the generals fought bloody wars of attrition, the diplomats on each side attempted to divide their enemies and achieve their governments' aims in less costly ways. The Allies concentrated primarily on probing the possibilities of a separate peace with Austria-Hungary, while Germany in turn tried similar tactics with Britain, France and Russia. Until 1917 the chances of a breakthrough were minimal. The Allies were handicapped in their dealings with Vienna by their lavish promises to Italy of territorial gains in Istria and Dalmatia at the expense of the Habsburg Empire. On the other side, the nature of Germany's war aims, which unambiguously entailed the German domination of Europe by force proved a major obstacle to peace, as it was this very threat that the Allies were fighting.

Only in 1917 did a constellation of factors emerge which initially favoured the prospects for a negotiated peace. In March 1917 the first Russian revolution occurred, bringing to power a liberal regime, which, while still committed to fighting, was under intense internal pressure from the Bolsheviks (Communists) to make peace. The growing hostility of the Russian people to a war fought for territorial gains in turn influenced labour movements throughout Europe to agitate for a compromise peace. In July the German *Reichstag* actually passed a resolution calling for a 'peace of understanding'. In April the United States entered the war as an Associated Power, rather than as an Ally. This ensured that she reserved her independence of action and could respond to peace initiatives as she thought fit. In Austria the aged and stubborn Franz-Josef had died in November 1916 and the new Emperor Charles was determined to secure a separate peace. Finally in the summer of 1917 the French army was paralysed by a series of mutinies on the western front. Surely here were the ideal preconditions for a negotiated peace?

There were three major peace initiatives. Charles approached the French through his French brother-in-law, Prince Sixte de Bourbon, in December 1916. In July the moderate wing of the international socialist movement invited socialists and labour representatives from all belligerent states to meet in Stockholm, and finally in August the Pope launched a peace programme calling for simultaneous disarmament and international arbitration. Why did none of these initiatives succeed and the war drag on until 1918? Essentially it was because the gap between the belligerents was still too wide. Germany, encouraged by the rapid weakening of Russia was determined to fight on, and her government increasingly fell under the influence of the generals, while Britain and France, now enormously strengthened by America's entry into the war both decided that ultimately victory was still possible. Thus to secure a peace with Austria, France was not ready to alienate her ally, Italy, by revising the Treaty of London in Austria's favour. Similarly neither Britain, France nor America would let their own labour delegates go to Stockholm for fear that this would trigger an unstoppable peace movement. By the autumn of 1917 Wilson was convinced that the defeat of the Central Powers was necessary before America could begin to take the lead in creating a new post-war world.

5 The Impact of the Bolshevik Revolution

In Russia the Bolsheviks overthrew the Provisional Government on 7 November 1917. This not only led to a three year civil war in which the Allies became involved but also gave the Germans their best chance of victory since August 1914. Lenin, the Bolshevik leader, although hoping that the revolution in Russia would trigger similar revolts throughout Europe, realised that if his regime was to survive he needed to make immediate peace with Germany. Thus on 22 December he began negotiations with the Germans at Brest-Litovsk after announcing to the world that he supported a peace without annexations or reparations. The Germans skilfully used Lenin's emphasis on self-determination to dictate a treaty creating a chain of apparently independent states, including the Ukraine, on Russia's eastern borders, which were in reality under German control. As the Allies refused to heed his calls for a general peace, Lenin had no option but to sign the Treaty of Brest-Litovsk on 3 March 1918.

Germany was now able to transfer large numbers of men and quantities of equipment across to the western front and on 21 March launched a major offensive in the West. Simultaneously she tightened her grip on western Russia and in August forced Lenin both to grant independence to Georgia and to guarantee the punctual delivery of oil supplies to Germany. The very scale of German successes in Russia faced the Allies with a whole number of new threats. By controlling large areas of western Russia not only would the Germans be able to weaken the Allied blockade, but they would be able to establish a strong Eurasian power bloc that would threaten British India and make Germany, even with American assistance to the Allies, virtually undefeatable. Since it was clear that Lenin was not prepared to risk war with the Germans, the Allies began to support the various anti-Bolshevik factions in the Russian civil war initially as a means of re-creating a second front. The British, French and the Americans could themselves only send small numbers of troops, but the interventionist forces were greatly strengthened by some 70,000 Japanese troops in eastern Siberia and by the revolt of the Czech legion which was made up of Czech deserters and prisoners of war from the Austro-Hungarian army. Once Germany was defeated in November 1918 the Allied forces were drawn deeper into the Russian civil war and their priority became the defeat of Bolshevism, or in the case of Japan, the creation of a new sphere of interest in eastern Siberia.

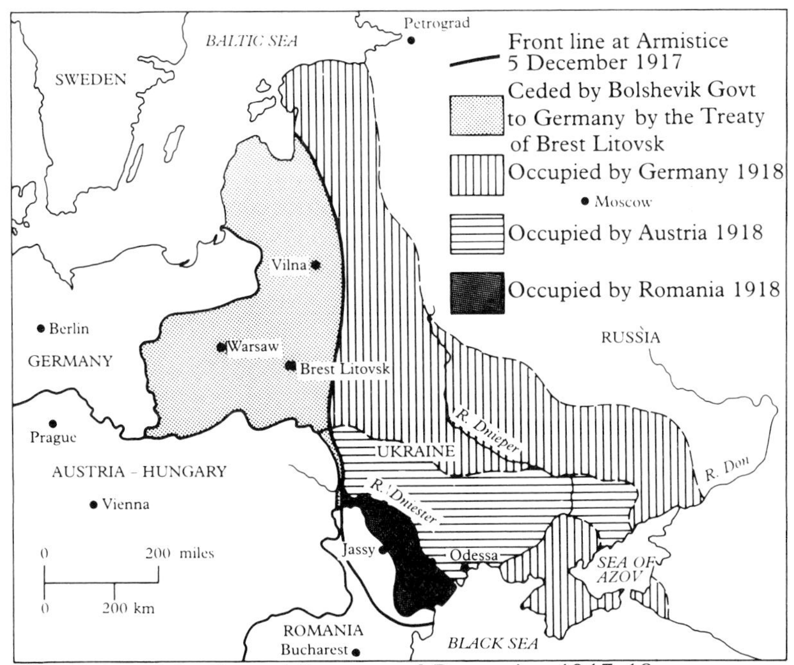

The Gains of the Central Powers and Romania, 1917-18

6 The Armistices of October and November 1918

The great German offensive of March 1918 had already been halted by July, and a month later the German High Command conceded that the war would have to be ended by negotiation, but after a moment of panic on 8 August when the British broke through the German lines, it still thought that it could negotiate from a position of reasonable strength. However, on 28 September after further military defeats in the west and Bulgaria's sudden request for a cease-fire in the east, the generals conceded defeat and advised the kaiser to form a new constitutional government, which would impress President Wilson with its democratic credentials and facilitate the negotiation of an armistice on the basis of the Fourteen Points. These had been announced by Wilson in January 1918 to the American Congress in response to Lenin's call for a peace without negotiations. They outlined American war aims and were to form the basis of American policy at the Paris Peace Conference in 1919. The Fourteen Points consisted of the following proposals:

1. Open covenants [agreements], openly arrived at ... diplomacy shall always proceed frankly and in the public view.
2. Absolute freedom of navigation upon the seas, outside territorial waters ...
3. The removal, so far as possible, of all economic barriers ...
4. Adequate guarantees given and taken that national armaments will be reduced to the lowest point consistent with domestic safety.
5. A free, open-minded, and absolutely impartial adjustment of all colonial claims ... the interests of the populations concerned must have equal weight with the equitable claims of the government whose title is to be determined.
6. The evacuation of all Russian territory ...
7. Belgium, the whole world will agree, must be evacuated and restored, without any attempt to limit the sovereignty, which she enjoys in common with all other free nations.
8. All French territory should be freed and the invaded portions restored, and the wrong done to France by Prussia in 1871 in the matter of Alsace Lorraine ... should be righted ...
9. A readjustment of the frontiers of Italy should be effected along clearly recognisable lines of nationality.
10. The peoples of Austria-Hungary, whose place among the nations we wish to see safeguarded and assured, should be accorded the freest opportunity of autonomous development.
11. Rumania, Serbia and Montenegro should be evacuated ... Serbia afforded free and secure access to the sea; and the relations of the several Balkan states to one another determined by friendly council along historically established

SOLDIER AND CIVILIAN.

MARSHAL FOCH (*to Messrs.* CLEMENCEAU, WILSON *and* LLOYD GEORGE). "IF YOU'RE GOING UP THAT ROAD, GENTLEMEN, LOOK OUT FOR BOOBY-TRAPS."

Soldier and Civilian, Punch *cartoon, 23 October 1918*

lines of allegiance and nationality ...

12 The Turkish portions of the present Ottoman empire should be assured a secure sovereignty, but the other nationalities ... should be assured an absolutely unmolested opportunity of autonomous development, and the Dardanelles should be permanently open as a free passage to the ships and commerce of all nations ...

13 An independent Poland should be erected which should include the territories inhabited by indisputably Polish populations, which should be assured a free and secure access to the sea ...

14 A general association of nations must be formed under specific covenants for the purpose of political independence and territorial integrity to great and small states alike ...

On 4 October the new German government asked Wilson for 'an immediate armistice' on the basis of the Fourteen Points. Similar requests then came from Austria-Hungary and the Ottoman Empire. Germany's hopes of dividing her enemies were dashed when Wilson then asked the Allies to draft the details of the armistice agreements. Despite the presence of Colonel House, Wilson's personal representative, the Allies rapidly secured a series of tough terms, which went far to protect their position at the coming Peace Conference: in the west the Germans were to evacuate all occupied territory, including Alsace-Lorraine and to withdraw beyond a 10 kilometre wide neutral zone to the east of the Rhine. Allied troops would then move in and occupy the west bank of the Rhine. In eastern Europe all German troops were similarly to be withdrawn from the occupied territories. The German navy was also to be interned in either a neutral or a British port. Paralysed by mutinies and strikes, which forced the abdication of the kaiser, the German government had little option but to accept the armistice on 11 November.

Austria-Hungary fared even worse. In the summer of 1918 America and the Allies had, in a desperate attempt to counter both German successes in eastern Europe and a joint Austro-German decision to create a permanent economic union, decided to abandon their former policy of dealing with Austria-Hungary as a sovereign state. Instead they recognised the right of her subject peoples, especially the Czechs and the Yugoslavs to independence. In Paris the exiled leaders of the Austrian Yugoslavs had already agreed to form a south Slav state (later to be called Yugoslavia), together with the Serbs, Croats and Slovenes. In October Wilson brushed aside attempts by Vienna to negotiate on behalf of its empire and the Czechs and Yugoslavs seized the chance to declare their independence. On 1 November the Austro-Hungarian union was dissolved and two days later the former Imperial High Command negotiated an armistice with the Italians. In the meantime the Turkish armistice was signed at Mudros on 30 October.

7 Conclusion

Why did the First World War last so long? Was it simply that once started, it gained a momentum of its own which no statesman could stop, or was it a titanic struggle over real issues that could only be solved on the battlefield? Lenin argued that the war was fought between rival capitalist systems for the control of the world's raw materials and economies. There is certainly an element of truth in Lenin's analysis. After all, for Great Powers, control over raw material supplies and ready access to a large free-trade zone to which they can profitably export are vital necessities for their existence. Does this mean therefore that there was little to choose between the two sides despite Allied propaganda claiming that they were fighting a war for the liberty of small nations? One leading historian of this period, David Stevenson, argues that 'submerged beneath the clash of rival imperialisms there was also an ideological contest between liberal and autocratic Powers'. It is probably true that a German victory would have ensured a more autocratic Europe than did the Allied and American settlements of 1919-20, but would the terms of an Allied victory before the entry of America into the war have been as liberal?

Making notes on *'The International Politics of the First World War'*

As you read this chapter try to identify the issues that divided the opposing powers. Ask yourself whether these issues remained the same throughout the war. To what extent do the official war aims of the Powers provide the key to this question? Why could the war not be stopped before November 1918? Were the politicians simply unable to stop the generals or were the Great Powers really engaged in a desperate struggle for survival? Your answer to these questions will be important for helping you to understand the policy of the Allies at the Peace Conference (chapter 3) and the issues discussed in the subsequent chapters leading up to the Second World War (chapters 4-6).

The following headings and sub-headings should help provide you with a useful framework for your notes:

1 The Outbreak of War, June-August 1914 - the sequence of events from the assassination of Franz Ferdinand to Britain's declaration of war, 28 June-4 August.

2 Why does the conflict widen and what are the motives for the entry of first Japan and Turkey and then Italy, the Balkan states and finally America into the conflict?

3.1 Outline the British, French and Russian war aims. To what extent did they clash with each other particularly in the Middle East?

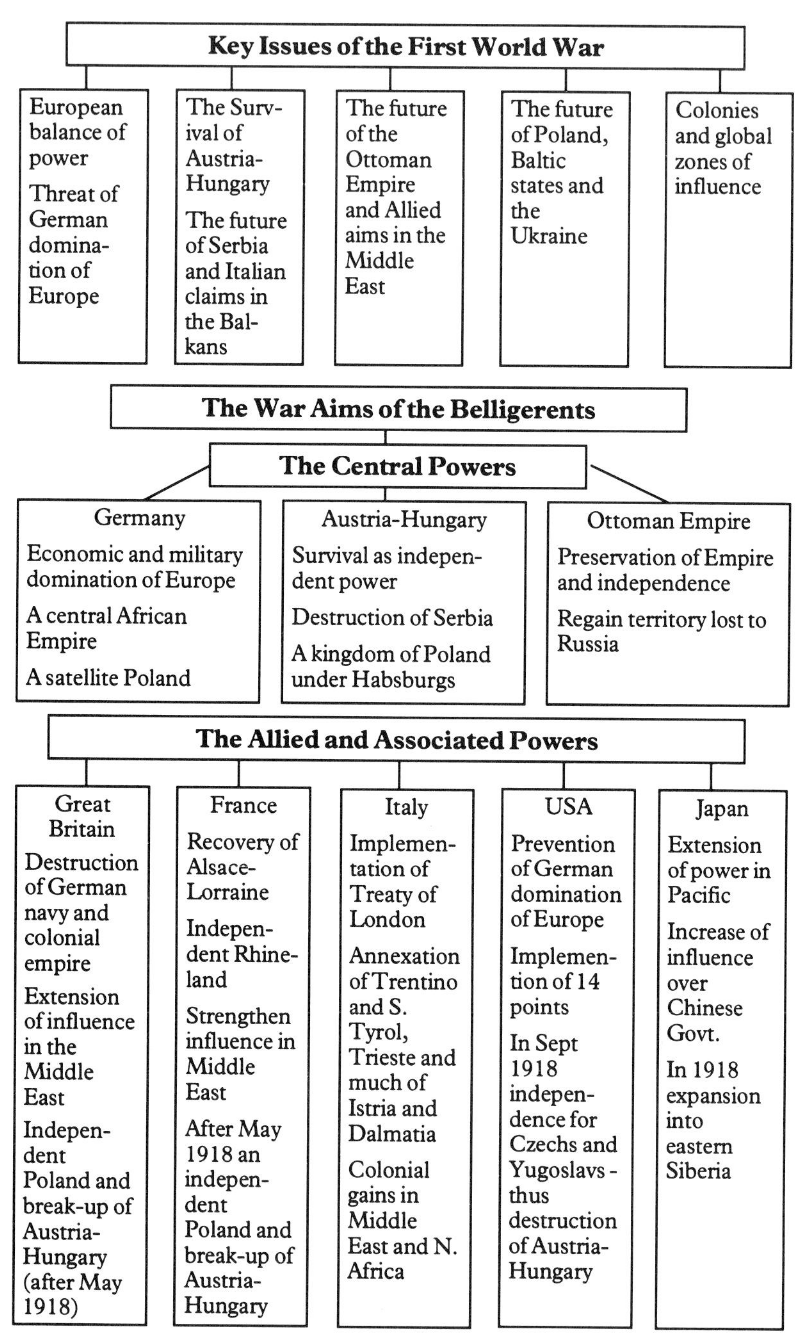

Summary - The International Politics of the First World War

3.2 Did Germany's war aims in essence boil down to the domination of Europe?
4 What attempts were there to reach a negotiated settlement, 1914-17 and why did they fail?
5.1 What was the impact of the Bolshevik Revolution and the Treaty of Brest-Litovsk on the international politics of the war?
5.2 Why did the Allies intervene militarily in Russia in 1918?
6 The Armistices
6.1 Why did the Germans appeal to Wilson on 4 October?
6.2 The German armistice
6.3 The Austro-Hungarian and Turkish armistices.

Answering essay questions on *'The International Politics of the First World War'*

Most questions set on this topic avoid concentrating on the diplomacy of only one Power. They tend to fall into two main categories: i) general questions on war aims and why the war lasted so long; ii) more specific questions on the 'turning point' of 1917. Thus candidates need to have firm ideas backed up with factual knowledge about why the Great Powers went to war, what their subsequent war aims were and why no compromise was possible until Germany was facing defeat in the Autumn of 1918.

Study the following questions:

1. How valid is the view that all the major Powers waged war between 1914-18 for defensive reasons?
2. 'Essentially the First World War was a battle between rival imperialist Powers seeking either to preserve their existing empires or to create new ones.' Discuss.
3. Why did the First World War go on for so long?
4. How did the events of 1917 influence the course and outcome of the First World War?

Questions on the international politics of the First World War can be specific, or more ambiguously worded. The specific question usually asks you bluntly to account for why or how something happened. The basic way to answer this is to plan a series of paragraphs each putting forward a different reason. However, just because these questions are straight forward be careful that your essay answer does not read to the examiner as if you have simply slapped down a list of facts that you have learnt off by heart but do not really understand. You must explore the cause and effect of relevant actions and events and not hesitate to indicate, as is usually the case in History, where causes and consequences are disputed. When this happens the examiner will always be impressed if you have made up your own mind as to which explanation you think is the most valid. The other, arguably more difficult, type of question puts forward a controversial quotation or opinion and asks you to discuss or assess it. The examiner does not expect you to agree with it. Your task will be to analyse it to see whether it provides clues to understanding the events it refers to, while possibly also showing that its interpretation is in many ways inaccurate.

Try now to relate this more general advice to the essay questions listed above. Questions 1 and 2 are primarily concerned with war aims. In both the examiner asks you to consider a possible major reason why the Great Powers fought. As a first step you should draw up a list of reasons covering both why the Powers went to war (see chapter 1 and Lowe, *Rivalry and Accord. International relations, 1870-1914, Access to History* series, chapter 5) and what kept them fighting for so long. You should certainly examine the explanations put forward by the examiner, but you should also provide others, backed up of course with evidence. In question 1 ask yourself at what point did the aims of the Great Powers go beyond the defensive. Could one argue that the Germany's September Programme and Britain's ambitions in the Middle East were 'defensive'? Question 2 neatly divides the belligerents into the 'haves' and 'have nots' and invites you to explore whether this is a valid explanation of the war. An examiner would expect you to show that the argument was not as simple as that. Questions 3 and 4 are more direct questions, but in both you must be careful of not falling into the trap of just telling the story of the war or of that crucial year 1917. Question 4 above all requires a detailed and accurate knowledge of the events of 1917 and 1918 which would have to be used analytically rather than in a narrative way.

Source-based questions on *'The International Politics of the First World War'*

1 French, German and Italian War Aims

Carefully read the extracts from Bülow's report on page 11, Briand's letter to Cambon of January 1917 on page 14 and from the 'September Programme' of 1914 on page 15. Answer the following questions:

a) What plans does Briand have in mind for the future of the Rhineland? (2 marks)
b) Explain the meaning of 'her domination over non-Russian vassal peoples broken' (page 15 line 5). (2 marks)
c) What was the 'indispensable minimum' (lines 6/7) that Italy demanded from the Central Powers? (4 marks)
d) Using these extracts and any other evidence known to you consider the view that Germany, France and Italy were all following similarly expansionist policies. Explain your answer fully. (12 marks)

2 The Fourteen Points

Carefully read the extract from the Fourteen Points on pages 18 and 20 and answer the following questions:

a) Explain the meaning of the second point. Against which Power or Powers was it directed? (3 marks)
b) What are the implications of the tenth point for the continued existence of Austria-Hungary? In answering this consider whether any of the other points are relevant. (5 marks)
c) Read the Fourteen Points through carefully. In what way do they help explain why the Germans hoped to negotiate an armistice with Wilson rather than with the Allies? Explain your answer fully. (7 marks)

3 The Armistice with Germany

Study carefully the cartoon on page 19 and answer the following questions:

a) Why is Marshal Foch portrayed as such a significant figure? (2 marks)
b) What is meant by 'Armistice Road' and what are the 'booby traps' on it that Foch is likely to have in mind? (7 marks)
c) In drawing up the Armistice terms how did the Allies protect themselves against these possible 'booby traps'? (6 marks)

CHAPTER 3

The Peace Settlements and the New Europe, 1919-23

1 Problems Facing the Peacemakers

In January 1919 the statesmen of the victorious powers were confronted with a Europe in turmoil. The problems facing them were infinitely more complex than those with which their predecessors in Vienna had grappled in 1814 in the aftermath of the Napoleonic Wars, and were not susceptible to simple solutions. In 1814 Europe had reached the end of the revolutionary cycle, which started with the outbreak of the French Revolution in 1789, and longed for stability. In 1919, as Lloyd George perceived,

> The situation is very different .... The whole of Russia is filled with a spirit of revolution ... the whole existing order in its political, social and economic aspects is questioned by the masses of the population from one end of Europe to another.

The sudden and complete defeat of the Central Powers had made Europe vulnerable to the spread of Communism from Russia. Germany for much of the winter of 1918-19 seemed poised on the brink of revolution. With the disintegration of the Habsburg, Ottoman and Romanov empires there seemed to be no stable government anywhere east of the Rhine. In March when the Communist leader, Bela Kun, seized power in Hungary, the French newspaper, *Echo de Paris,* declared that 'the door to the heart of Europe' was now open to Communism.

Nor in eastern Europe and the Balkans did the end of hostilities between the Central Powers and the Allies lead to peace. At the railheads the Habsburg armies disintegrated, and Magyars, Poles, Czechs and Slavs fought with each other to seize weapons and munitions with which to equip their embryonic national armies and gain crucial territorial advantages in the struggle to set up new national states in the vacuum created by collapse of Austia-Hungary and the defeat of Germany. In the Baltic the Red Armies exploited the partial retreat of the Germans to occupy Lithuania and Latvia.

The fear of revolution was intensified by the influenza pandemic which by the spring of 1919 had caused the deaths of millions of people, and by the near famine conditions in central and eastern Europe. Even in the British occupied zone in the Rhineland, where the inhabitants were better fed than in unoccupied Germany, a nutrition expert described the daily food ration 'as not enough to live on and too much to die on'. The problems facing the statesmen in Paris were thus not only the negotiation of peace and the drawing up of new frontiers, but also the pressing need to avert economic chaos and famine. As one Allied official observed, 'there was a veritable race between peace and anarchy'.

The task of rebuilding a peaceful and prosperous Europe was made more difficult by the continued strength of nationalist feeling amongst the populations of the victorious powers. Nationalist opinion in Britain, America, France and Italy viewed the peace conference as the final phase of the war in which their leaders must ruthlessly consolidate the gains made on the battlefields and smash the enemy for ever. Public opinion in the Allied nations and even in the United States turned decisively against a policy of conciliation. Everywhere the moderates lost ground. The greatest blow to the prospects for real peace in Europe were delivered when the Congressional elections in America in November 1918 gave the Republicans a majority. The Republicans were determined to campaign for a hard peace with Germany and simultaneously insist that America should neither become involved in guaranteeing it nor in financing any expensive schemes for European reconstruction. Thus there was little chance that America would agree to share the costs of rebuilding the French and Belgium economies in an act of self-interested generosity that might have anticipated the financial help America gave western Europe after the Second World War under the Marshall Plan of 1947.

2 Aims and Principles of the Great Powers

The peace negotiations at Paris are often interpreted as a struggle between the proponents of reconciliation, led by Wilson and Lloyd George, and the ruthless advocates of a peace of revenge represented by Clemenceau, the French Prime Minister. While there is some truth in this analysis, it simplifies the divisions amongst the peacemakers in Paris. Not only were the great powers divided in their objectives at Paris, but their individual peace programmes also in themselves contained contradictory policies. It is not always accurate to regard the French as pursuing revenge, while the British and Americans followed the more noble aims of peace and reconciliation. Wilson strongly believed that Germany needed to be punished for her part in starting the war and that she should be put on 'probation' before joining the League. In a speech at Omaha on 18 September 1919 he declared that the Treaty of Versailles:

1 seeks to punish one of the greatest wrongs ever done in history, the wrong which Germany sought to do to the world and to civilisation, and there ought to be no weak purpose with regard to punishment. She attempted an intolerable thing, and she must be
5 made to pay for the attempt.

Wilson was determined to ensure that the Fourteen Points (see pages 18-20) would serve as a basis for the coming peace negotiations and anchor the Covenant (or constitution) of the League of Nations in the text of the peace treaties. There was broad general agreement amongst the victors to approve the creation of independent national states in eastern Europe and the Balkans and confine Turkey to her ethnic frontiers, all of which was anticipated by points 10-13. Points 7 and 8, covering the liberation of Belgium and the return of Alsace-Lorraine to France, had already been fulfilled at the start of the Armistice, while some of the other Points, the complete realisation of which would have created serious tensions between America and the Allies, were the subject of discrete compromise by Washington. Britain, for instance was assured that point 2, which demanded the 'freedom of the seas', did not mean the immediate lifting of the blockade against Germany. The French and Belgians were promised American support for German reparations despite the absence of any such clause in the Fourteen Points, and Italy, the award of former Austrian territory up to the Brenner frontier even though this would include over 200,000 Germans. Wilson was also ready to compromise with Britain over the former German colonies and the Middle Eastern possessions of Turkey. These territories would be the ultimate responsibility of the new League of Nations but would be handed over as mandates to the appropriate powers to administer. The British ambassador in Washington was specifically reassured by Wilson's adviser, Colonel House, that since Britain had pioneered the fairest colonial system in the world, she would therefore be an ideal mandatory power.

These concessions did not go far enough to turn the Fourteen Points into a practicable inter-Allied consensus for the coming peace negotiations. They failed to overcome imperialist rivalries between Britain and France in the Middle East or between America, Japan and Britain in the Far East. Nor, as will be seen, did they provide a solution to the rival claims in 1919-20 of Italy and the new 'kingdom of the Serbs, Croats and Slovenes' (which later became Yugoslavia) to Dalmatia .

More importantly they failed to impress the French Premier, Clemenceau, who was convinced that only an effective balance of power in Europe could contain Germany. He was painfully aware that France, with its reduced birthrate and a total number of casualties of 1.3 million dead and another 2.8 million wounded, faced a Germany which, as a consequence of the collapse of Austria-Hungary and Tsarist Russia, was potentially stronger than in 1914. He told the French parliament in December 1918:

1 There was an old system which seems condemned today and to which I do not hesitate to say that I remain to some extent faithful: nations organise their defence. It was very prosaic. They tried to have strong frontiers ... . This system seems condemned today by

> 5 the very high authorities Yet I believe that if this balance, which had been spontaneously produced during the war, had existed earlier: if, for example, England, America and Italy had agreed in saying that whoever attacked one of them had attacked the whole world, this war would never have taken place.

Clemenceau was anxious to enforce maximum disarmament on the Germans, to encourage a large independent Poland, and viable Czechoslovak and Yugoslav states, once it became clear that he could not rely on the restoration of Imperial Russia to restrain Germany, and to create an independent Rhineland state. He also intended to extract reparation payments from Germany. His main priority, however, was to retain the wartime links with Britain and America and to continue inter-Allied financial and economic co-operation into the post-war years. He was ready to make considerable concessions to do this. For instance, in December 1918 in the Middle East Clemenceau was prepared to cede Palestine and the Mosul oil fields to the British in the hope of gaining their support in Europe.

In contrast to France, Britain, even before the Great Powers met in Paris, had already achieved many of her aims: the German fleet had surrendered, German trade rivalry was no longer a threat and Germany's colonial empire was liquidated, while the German armies in western Europe had been driven back into the Reich. Britain's territorial ambitions lay in the Middle East, not Europe. In January 1919 Lloyd George envisaged the preservation of a peaceful united Germany as a barrier against Bolshevism. Above all he wanted to avoid long-term British commitments on the continent of Europe and prevent the annexation of German minorities by the Poles or the French creating fresh areas of bitterness which would sow the seeds of a new war. Inevitably then these objectives were fundamentally opposed to the French policy of securing definite guarantees against a German military revival either by negotiating a long-term Anglo-American military alliance or by a partial dismemberment of the German empire.

The logic of British policy pointed in the direction of a peace of reconciliation rather than revenge, but in two key areas, reparations and the question of German war guilt, Britain adopted a more intransigent line. Lloyd George and Clemenceau agreed in December 1918 that the kaiser should be tried by an international tribunal for war crimes. Under pressure from the Dominions, who also wanted a share of reparations, the British Delegation at Paris was authorised:

> to endeavour to secure from Germany the greatest possible indemnity she can pay consistently with the well being of the British Empire and the peace of the world without involving an army of occupation in Germany for its collection.

The aims of both Japan and Italy were concentrated on maximising their war-time gains. Orlando, the Italian Prime Minister, was anxious to convince the voters that Italy had done well out of the war, and concentrated initially on attempting to hold the Entente to their promises made in the Treaty of London (see page 11), as well as demanding the port of Fiume in the Adriatic. Japan, for whom the war had provided marvellous opportunities to seize both the German islands in the Pacific and their treaty rights in Shantung (see page 10) wanted recognition of her gains. She also pushed hard, but ultimately unsuccessfully, to have a racial equality clause included in the Covenant of the League of Nations. She hoped that this would protect Japanese immigrants in America.

Wilson's most immediate aim was to have the constitution or covenant of the League quickly drawn up ready to be incorporated into the Treaty. He was convinced that then 'nearly all the serious difficulties' at the peace conference would somehow disappear, as he assumed that this would automatically create a framework in which the other clauses of the treaties could be considered rationally. This was, however, to be a wildly optimistic assessment.

3 The Organisation of the Paris Peace Conference

Compared to the Vienna Congress of 1814-15, the Paris Conference was a show piece of sophisticated organisation. The British delegation, for instance, which was composed of 207 officials, as compared to a mere 17 in 1814, had its own printing press, telephone lines to London and the capitals of the Empire and a direct daily air link to Croydon airfield. Yet despite this impressive evidence of outward efficiency, the Conference got off to a slow start and for the first two months little progress was made towards a German settlement. The reasons for this were partly organisational and partly because the Allied statesmen rapidly discovered that they formed what Lloyd George called, a 'Cabinet of Nations', which could not ignore the pressing problems of immediate post-war Europe. They had to consider the emergency consignments of food to central and eastern Europe, set up the Supreme Economic Council to deal with the financial and economic problems affecting both occupied and unoccupied Germany and negotiate the easing of the food blockade of Germany in exchange for the surrender of the German merchant fleet. Above all they ceaselessly monitored the progress of the civil war in Russia and weighed up the pros and cons of Allied military intervention (see pages 44-5).

When the Peace Conference opened on 18 January 1919 the delegates of 27 states attended, but in reality power lay with the 'big five': Britain, France, Italy, Japan and the USA. Each, with the exception of Japan, which to a great extent relied on its professional diplomats, was at first represented by their wartime leaders in the

Council of Ten (two representatives per country). Neither Russia nor the defeated enemy powers attended. Lloyd George and Wilson had both attempted to secure Russian representation at Paris, but Allied efforts to negotiate a truce between the factions in the civil war failed when the Whites refused to attend a conference on the island of Prinkipo in the Sea of Mamara in February 1919. Right up to April the Allies were not sure whether to follow the pattern of previous peace conferences and plan for a preliminary peace with Germany and the other Central Powers, which would only contain the disarmament terms and the outlines of the territorial settlement; and then at a later date, when passions had cooled, call an international congress to which the ex-enemy states would be invited. Foch, the Supreme Allied Military Commander, was bitterly opposed to this scenario as he feared that the Germans would easily be able to exploit the tensions and rivalries between the Allies to gain major concessions.

Thus unsure in their own mind whether they were working on a preliminary or final treaty, the Council of Ten grappled with the intricate problems of peace-making. Fifty-eight committees were set up to draft the clauses of not only the German treaty but also the treaties with Austria, Bulgaria, Hungary and Turkey. Their work was handicapped by the absence of any central co-ordinating body and consequently the different committees worked in isolation from each other, sometimes coming up with contradictory solutions. It was not until 24 March that the organisation of the Conference was streamlined as a result of Lloyd George's controversial Fontainbleau Memorandum. Inspired by the fear that the Allies might drive Germany into the arms of the Bolsheviks, it urged major concessions to Berlin, which raised such important issues that they could only be resolved by secret discussions between Clemenceau, Lloyd George, Orlando and Wilson. This 'Council of Four' proved so effective that it became the key decision-making committee of the Conference. As most of the territorial committees had finished their reports, it was also decided to drop the idea of a preliminary peace and to proceed quickly to a final settlement with Germany, thereby abandoning the idea of a later congress and so minimising the opportunities for Germany to exploit inter-Allied differences at a time when the Allies were rapidly demobilising their armies.

Inevitably this decision had serious repercussions on the drafting of the treaty and possibly for the future peace of Europe. Harold Nicolson, a member of the British delegation at Paris, argued in 1933 that

> 1 Many paragraphs of the Treaty, and especially in the economic
> section were in fact inserted as 'maximum statements' such as
> would provide some area of concession to Germany at the eventual
> congress. This congress never materialised: the last weeks flew past
> 5 us in a hysterical nightmare; and these 'maximum statements'

remained unmodified and were eventually imposed by ultimatum.

On the other hand it is arguable that such were the problems the Allied statesmen faced in 1919 that, as Professor Beloff has observed, it is surprising 'not that the treaties were imperfect but that they were concluded at all'.

4 The Settlement with Germany

All peace settlements are to a greater or lesser extent the result of compromises between the negotiating powers. Versailles was no exception. Its key clauses were the result of fiercely negotiated agreements, which were often only reached when the conference appeared to be on the brink of collapse.

The first 26 articles (which appeared in all the other treaties as well) contained the Covenant of the League of Nations (see pages 66-8) and were agreed unanimously once Wilson had met French objections by initially excluding Germany from the League.

Despite some American and Italian reservations, which were eventually overcome by Lloyd George and Clemenceau, about the legality of demanding the surrender of the kaiser and other German leaders for trial for committing acts against 'the laws and customs of war', there was universal agreement amongst the victorious powers that Germany was guilty of having started the war .

It was this principle of war guilt, that was to provide the moral justification for the reparation clauses of the Treaty which was stressed in Article 231 of the Treaty:

> 1 The Allied and Associated Governments affirm and Germany accepts the responsibility of Germany and her allies for causing all the loss and damage to which the Allied and Associated Governments and their nationals have been subjected as a
> 5 consequence of the war imposed up them by the aggression of Germany and her allies.

Although there was general agreement that Germany should pay an indemnity to the victors, there was considerable debate about the amount she should pay, the nature of the damage deserving compensation and how Germany could raise such large sums of money without harming the Allied economies. Essentially the major issue behind the Allied demands was the compelling need to cover the costs of financing the war. Britain had covered one-third of its war expenditure through taxation, while France just one-sixth. At a time of severe social unrest no Allied country could easily face the prospect of financing debt repayments by huge tax increases and savage cuts in expenditure. Initially it was hoped that America could be persuaded to continue wartime inter-Allied economic co-operation and above all cancel the repayment of Allied war debts, but by the end of 1918 it was obvious that this was not going to happen as Wilson dissolved all the agencies for inter-Allied co-operation in Washington. Without American participation the British Treasury was reluctant to continue its wartime co-operation with the French Finance Ministry and in March 1919 all further financial assistance from Britain to France was stopped. France had no option therefore but to seek financial reparation from Germany. The French appeared to have operated on two levels. The French finance minister, Louis Klotz, backed by the press and the Chamber of Deputies, urged a policy of maximum claims, and coined the slogan that 'Germany will pay' (for everything). Behind the scenes, however, Loucheur, the Minister for Reconstruction, pursued a more subtle policy and informed the Germans that such was the need of the French economy for an immediate injection of cash, that his government would settle for a more moderate sum, which the Germans would be able to raise quickly through the sale of bonds on the world's financial markets. The German government, however, suspected that these overtures were merely a means of dividing Germany from America, which was seen in Berlin as the country potentially most sympathetic to the German cause. America's reparation policy was certainly more moderate than either Britain's or France's as it recommended that a modest fixed sum should be written into the Treaty.

The British delegation consistently maximised their country's reparation claims on Germany. Some historians explain this in terms of the pressure exerted on the government by the electorate. On the other hand Lloyd George himself claimed that 'the imposition of a high indemnity ... would prevent the Germans spending money on an army'. It was arguable that a high indemnity would also ensure that there would be money left over for Britain and the Dominions after France and Belgium had claimed their share. To safeguard Britain's percentage of reparations, the Imperial War Cabinet urged that the cost of war pensions should be included in the reparation bill. By threatening to walk out of the Conference, Lloyd George then forced the Council of Four to support his arguments. The British pension claims made it even more difficult for the Allied financial experts to agree on an overall figure for reparations. Consequently, at the end of April, it was agreed that the Reparation Commission should be set up to assess in detail by 1 May 1921 what the German economy could afford. In the meantime, the Germans would make an interim payment of 20 milliard or (American) billion gold marks and raise a further 60 milliard through the sale of bonds. It was not until December 1919 that Britain and France agreed on the ratio 25:55 respectively as the percentage of the total reparations which each power should eventually receive. Belgium was the only power to be awarded full compensation for her losses and priority in payment of the first sums due from Germany, largely because she too, threatened to withdraw from the Conference in May at a time when Italy had already walked out and the Japanese were also threatening to do so.

As with reparations, the Allied and Associated nations agreed on the necessity for German disarmament, but there were differences in emphasis. The British and Americans wished to destroy in Germany the tradition of conscription, which they regarded as 'the taproot of militarism', while Foch, more wisely as it turned out, feared that a professional army would become a tightly organised cadre force which would be capable of quick expansion when the opportunity arose. Foch was overruled and the Council of Ten accepted in March proposals for the creation of inter-Allied commissions to monitor the pace of German disarmament, the abolition of the General Staff, the creation of a regular army of 100,000 men, the dissolution of the airforce and the reduction of the navy to a handful of ships.

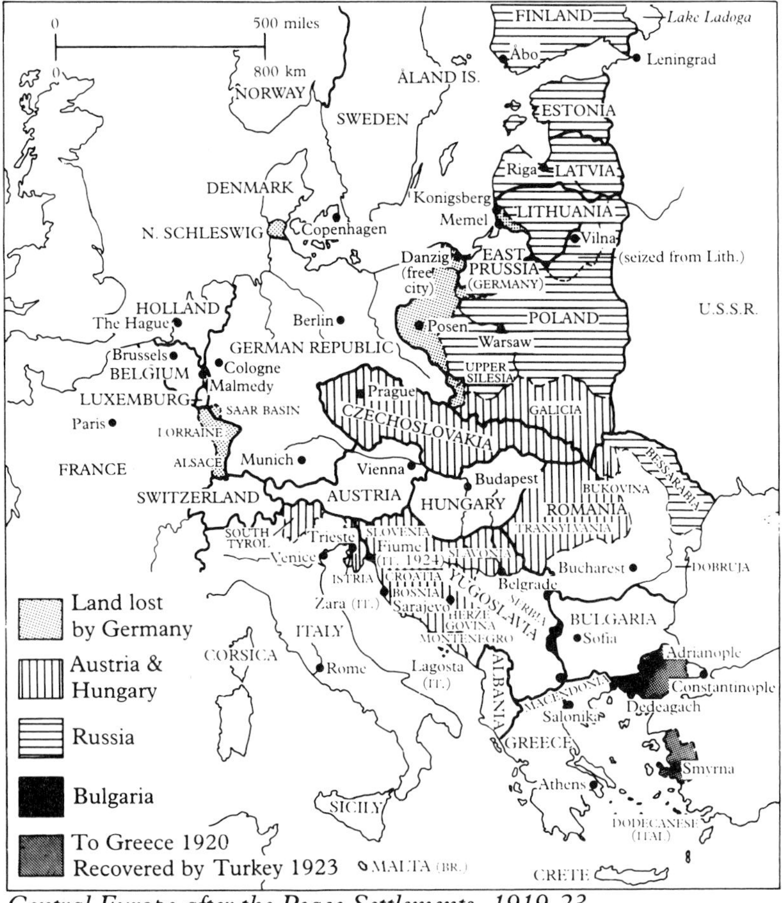

Central Europe after the Peace Settlements, 1919-23

It was accepted, even by many Germans, that the predominantly Danish northern Schleswig, annexed by Bismarck in 1866, should be returned to the Danes. There was therefore general agreement that a plebiscite should be held to determine the size of the area to be handed back. The former German territories of Eupen and Malmedy, together with Moresnet, which before 1914 had been administered jointly by Germany and Belgium, were ceded to Belgium, and the neutrality of the Grand Duchy of Luxemburg was confirmed.

The French proposals for the future of the Saarland proved more controversial. Clemenceau insisted on the restoration to France of that part of the Saar which was given to Prussia in 1814. He also aimed to detach the mineral and industrial basin to the north, which had never been French and place it under an independent non-German administration. Finally he demanded full French ownership of the coal mines on both sides of the frontier to compensate for the destruction of the pits in the Nord and Pas-de-Calais by the Germans. Wilson immediately perceived that here was a clash between the national interests of France and the principle of self-determination as enshrined in the Fourteen Points. While he was ready to agree to French access to the coal mines until the production of their own mines had been restored, he categorically vetoed the other demands. To save the Conference from breaking down Lloyd George persuaded Wilson and Clemenceau to accept a compromise whereby the mines would become French, while the actual government of the Saar would be entrusted to the league. After 15 years the people would have the right to decide in a plebiscite whether they wished to return to German rule.

Over the future of the Rhineland there was an equally bitter clash between Britain and France. The British had no ambitions on the Rhine, but to the French the occupation of the Rhine was a unique opportunity to weaken Germany permanently by detaching the whole area from her. The British feared that not only would this create a new area of tension between France and Germany but that it would tilt the balance of power in Europe decisively towards France. Only after heated and often bitter arguments was a compromise at last reached. Clemenceau agreed to limit the Allied occupation of the Rhineland to a 15-year period in return for an Anglo-American treaty guaranteeing France against a new German attack. The Rhineland would be divided into three zones, each of which would be evacuated after 5 years. Thereafter the Rhineland would be a demilitarised zone barred to German troops, but under German administration. Lloyd George was unwilling to accept even this length of occupation and right up to the signature of the Treaty he sought to evade the commitment.

Anglo-French disagreements again dominated negotiations on Germany's eastern frontiers. The Commission on Polish Affairs recommended on 12 March that Danzig, Marienwerder and Upper Silesia should all be included in the new Polish state and that the future of Allenstein should be decided by plebiscite. Lloyd George vigorously opposed the inclusion of Danzig and Marienwerder as he feared the long-term resentment of the local and predominantly German speaking population and dreaded that an embittered Berlin might turn to Bolshevik Russia for help. By threatening to withdraw from the Anglo-American guarantee pact, he forced Clemenceau to agree to the holding of a plebiscite in Marienwerder and the establishment of a free and autonomous city of Danzig to be linked with Poland by a customs union and presided over by a High Commissioner appointed by the League of Nations.

President Wilson was adamant that the League should also have ultimate control over the former German colonies. This was accepted only reluctantly by the British Dominions of New Zealand, Australia and South Africa, each arguing that the outright annexation by themselves of the South Pacific islands, Samoa and South West Africa was vital for Imperial security. In May agreement was reached on the division of the German colonies. Britain, France and South Africa were allocated most of the former German colonial empire in Africa, while Australia, New Zealand and Japan secured the mandates for the scattered German possessions in the Pacific. Italy was awarded control of the Juba valley in East Africa, and a few minor territorial adjustments were made to her Libyan frontier with Algeria. Essentially Britain, the Dominions and France had secured what they wanted, despite paying lip-service to the League by agreeing to mandate status for the former German colonies.

A more serious clash arose between Japan and America. The Japanese were determined to hold on to the ex-German leasehold territory of Kiaochow in Shantung in China. The Chinese government, however, on the strength of its declaration of war against Germany in 1917 argued that all former German rights should automatically revert to the Chinese state, despite the fact that in 1915 it had agreed to recognise Japanese rights in Shantung. Wilson was anxious to block the growth of Japanese influence in the Pacific and supported China, but Lloyd George and Clemenceau, wanting to protect their own rights in China backed Japan. Wilson, already locked in conflict with the Italians over their claims to Fiume (see pages 40-1), and facing Japanese threats to boycott the Conference and sign a separate peace with Germany, had no option but to concede. It is arguable that this humiliating defeat did much to turn the American Senate against the treaty of Versailles.

While the Allies were working on the Treaty, the German government was totally isolated and could only prepare for the time when it would be summoned to Paris to receive the draft treaty.

On 7 May the draft peace terms were at last presented to the Germans who were given a mere 15 days to draw up their reply. The German government accepted much of the Treaty, but they did demand some significant concessions: immediate membership of the League of

Nations, a guarantee that Austria and the ethnic Germans in the Sudetenland, which was a part of the new Czechslovak state, should have the chance to decide whether they wished to join Germany, and finally the setting up of a neutral commission to examine the war guilt question.

These demands, which if met, might have greatly strengthened Germany in the post-war world, were rejected outright by the Allied and Associated Powers, but nevertheless some ground was conceded. Lloyd George, fearful that war might break out again, managed to persuade the French to agree to an eventual plebiscite in Upper Silesia. He failed to limit the Rhineland occupation to five years, but did manage to secure the vague assurance which later became Article 431 of the Treaty 'that once Germany had given concrete evidence of her willingness to fulfil her obligations', the Allied and Associated Powers would consider 'an

THE RECKONING.

PAN-GERMAN. "MONSTROUS, I CALL IT. WHY, IT'S FULLY A QUARTER OF WHAT *WE* SHOULD HAVE MADE *THEM* PAY, IF *WE'D* WON."

The Reckoning, Punch *cartoon, 23 April 1919*

earlier termination of the period of occupation'.

On 16 June the Germans were handed the final version of the Treaty incorporating these concessions. Not surprisingly, given the depth of opposition to it amongst the German people, it triggered a political crisis splitting the Cabinet and leading to the resignation of the Chancellor. Yet in view of its own military weakness, the Berlin Government had little option but to accept the Treaty, although it made very clear that it was acting under duress:

> 1 ... Surrendering to superior force but without retracting its opinion regarding the unheard of injustice of the peace conditions, the government of the German Republic therefore declares its readiness to accept and sign the peace conditions imposed by the
> 5 Allied and Associated Governments.

On 28 June the Treaty was signed in the Hall of Mirrors at Versailles where in 1871 the German Empire had been proclaimed. By January 1920 it had been ratified by all the signatory powers with the important exception of America. In Washington crucial amendments had been put forward by a coalition of isolationists, led by senators Lodge and Borah, rejecting the Shantung settlement and seriously modifying the Covenant of the League. The isolationists objected to the right of the British Dominions to vote as separate members in the League and were determined to subject America's obligation to defend the independence of fellow League members from aggression to strict control by Congress. They also proposed that Congress should be empowered to veto American participation in any League initiative that clashed with America's traditional policy, laid down in the Monroe Doctrine, of excluding foreign intervention from the American hemisphere. Wilson felt that these amendments would paralyse the League and so refused to accept them. He failed twice to secure the necessary 2/3 majority in the Senate. It was a major defeat for Wilson, and the consequences for Europe were serious. Without American ratification the Anglo-American military guarantee of France lapsed and the burden of carrying out the Treaty of Versailles was mainly to fall upon Britain and France.

5 The South Eastern European Settlements

After the ceremony at Versailles the Allied leaders returned home leaving their officials to draft the treaties with Germany's former allies. The outlines of a settlement in eastern Europe and the Balkans were already clear: Austria-Hungary and the Romanov empire had collapsed, the Poles and Czechs had declared their independence and the South Slavs had decided to federate with Serbia to form what was later to be called Yugoslavia. The bewildering diversity of races in the Balkans which, were in no way concentrated in easily definable areas, would ensure that however the Great Powers drew the frontiers the final settlement would be full of anomalies. The three defeated powers, Austria, Hungary, (who were both treated as the heirs to the former Habsburg Empire), and Bulgaria, all had to pay reparations, disarm and submit to the humiliation of a war guilt clause.

The basis of the settlement in south central Europe and the Balkans was the creation of the new Czecho-Slovak state and Serbo-Croat-Slovene state, or Yugoslavia. The Treaty of St Germain signed on 10 September 1919 split up the federation of territories which before the war had been part of Austria. Italy was awarded South Tyrol, despite the existence there of some 230,000 ethnic Germans, while Bohemia and Moravia were ceded to Czechoslovakia. Any reservations the British or Americans had about handing over to the Czechs the three million Germans, who made up nearly a third of the population of these provinces, was overcome by French insistence. The French wanted a potential ally against Germany to be strengthened by a defensible frontier and the possession of the Pilsen munitions works, both of which entailed the forcible integration of large German minorities into Czechoslovakia. They were also reassured by the promises of 'the honey tongued' (A.W. Palmer) Benes, the Czech representative at Paris, that his government would make Czechoslovakia a racially harmonious federal republic like Switzerland. Slovenia, Bosnia-Herzegovina and Dalmatia were handed over to Yugoslavia while Galicia and Bukovina were ceded respectively to Poland and Romania. Only in Carinthia where the population consisted of German speaking Slovenes, who did not want to join Yugoslavia, did the Great Powers consent to a plebiscite. This resulted in 1920 in the area remaining Austrian. To avoid the dangers of an Austrian union with Germany, Article 88 (which was identical with Article 80 in the Treaty of Versailles) stated that only the Council of the League of Nations was empowered to sanction a change in Austria's status as an independent state. Effectively this meant that France could veto any proposed change. Of all the defeated powers in 1919 it is arguable that Hungary suffered the most severely. By the Treaty of Trianon she lost over two thirds of her territory and 41.6 per cent of her population. In an age of nationalism she was particularly vulnerable to partition, as essentially only the heart lands of Hungary, the great Central Plain, were Magyar. Her eventual near dismemberment was signalled when, in November 1918 Serb, Czech and Romanian troops all occupied the regions they claimed. The completion of the treaty was delayed by Bela Kun's coup in March (see page 26). He succeeded in driving out the Czechs from eastern Slovakia, but was himself defeated by Romanian troops in August. Negotiations with the new Hungarian government were resumed in January 1920 and concluded in June. Most of the German speaking area in the west of the former Hungarian state was ceded to Austria, the Slovakian and Ruthenian regions in the north went to Czechoslovakia, the east to

Romania and the south to Yugoslavia. The Treaty of Trianon was justified by the Allies according to the principle of self-determination, but in the context of Hungary this was a principle almost impossible to realise. C.A. Macartney, an expert on Hungary and the successsor states, observed in 1937:

> 1 ... the ethnical line was practically nowhere clear cut ... long centuries of interpenetration, assimilation, migration and internal colonisation had left in many places a belt of mixed and often indeterminate population where each national group merged into
> 5 the next, while there were innumerable islands of one nationality set in seas of another, ranging in size from the half-million of Magyar speaking Szekely in Transylvania through many inter-determinate groups of fifty or a hundred thousand down to communities of a single village or less. ... No frontier could be
> 10 drawn which did not leave national minorities on at least one side of it.

Wherever there was a clash of interests between Hungary and the successor states or Romania, the Allies ensured that the decision went against Hungary.

This same principle operated in the negotiations leading up to the Treaty of Neuilly with Bulgaria, which was signed in November 1919. Essentially Britain and France regarded Bulgaria as 'the Balkan Prussia' which needed to be restrained. They were determined, despite reservations from Italy and America, to reward their allies, Romania, Greece and Serbia (now part of Yugoslavia) at its expense. Thus southern Dobruja, with a mere 7000 Romanians out of a total population of a quarter of a million was ceded to Romania and western Thrace was given to Greece.

The settlements were often accompanied by bitter quarrels between nominal allies. The Poles and the Czechs, for example, fought for the control of Teschen in early 1919 and the Yugoslavs and Romanians argued heatedly about their rival claims to the Banat. The most serious clash of opinions took place between Italy and America over Italian claims to Dalmatia and Fiume. Orlando and Sonnino were desperate to prove to their electorate that Italy was not a 'proletarian nation' which could be dictated to by the Great Powers, and therefore at first insisted that the Treaty of London of May 1915 should be honoured in full. They also wished to annex Albania and the port of Fiume in which it could be argued that there was a bare majority of ethnic Italians if the Croat suburb of Susak was conveniently left out of the picture. The Italian annexation of Fiume would also have the added bonus of denying Yugoslavia its only effective port in the Adriatic, thereby strengthening Italy's economic grip on the region. As Britain and France were reluctantly ready to honour the Treaty of London, an agreement could probably have been achieved, especially as Orlando in April 1919 indicated that he would be willing to accept Fiume as a compromise for renouncing Italian claims on Dalmatia. Wilson then made the major political mistake of vetoing the compromise publicly in a statement in the French press. After compromising over the Saar and Shantung, Wilson was stubbornly determined to make a stand on the Fourteen Points in the Adriatic. Orlando and Sonnino walked out of the Peace Conference in protest and did not return until 9 May. Orlando's resignation and his replacement by Nitti in June opened the way up for secret negotiations in Paris, but the lynching of nine French troops in Fiume by an Italian mob in July and then the seizure of the city in September by the Italian nationalist poet, d'Annunzio, merely prolonged the crisis. An agreement was reached in 1920 once the Yugoslavs realised that Wilson lacked the domestic support to interfere in the details of the Balkan settlements and when the Italian government, anxious to concentrate on Italy's pressing social and economic problems, showed its willingness to compromise by pulling its troops out of Albania. In November 1920 Yugoslavia and Italy signed the Treaty of Rapallo. Istria was partitioned between the two powers, Fiume became a self-governing free city and the rest of Dalmatia went to Yugoslavia. In December Italian troops cleared d'Annunzio out of Fiume, but in late 1923 Mussolini reoccupied it.

6 The Settlement with Turkey, 1919-23

Of all the treaties negotiated in 1919-20, the Treaty of Sèvres, signed on 10 August 1920 was the most obvious failure as it was never put into effect by the Turkish government. It can be argued that Sèvres was essentially an anachronism aimed at solving the 'Eastern Question' - the problem posed by the decline of Turkish power in the eastern Mediterranean, which had ceaselessly preoccupied the Great Powers in the century up to 1914, and that it took little account of the profound changes in Turkey brought about by the rise of Mustapha Kemal, the leader of the new nationalist movement. Kemal had set up a rebel government, which controlled virtually the whole of the Turkish interior, and was determined not to accept the Treaty of Sèvres . Only if the Treaty had been imposed within the first few months of the Turkish defeat before Kemal had built up support, might it have been successful, but the long delay until August 1920 ensured that growing Turkish resentment particularly at the Greek occupation of Smyrna, which the Allies had encouraged in May 1919, made its enforcement an impossibility.

The Treaty of Sèvres was an Anglo-French compromise. Lloyd George hoped drastically to weaken Turkey by depriving it not only of Constantinople and of the control of the Straits, but also by forcing it to surrender all territories where arguably there was no ethnic Turkish majority. He now envisaged Greece, rather than Italy (see page 14), filling the vacuum left by the collapse of Turkish power and in effect becoming the agent of the British Empire in the eastern Mediterranean. The French, on the other hand, concerned to protect their pre-war investments in Turkey, wished to preserve a viable Turkish state. Above all they wanted the Turkish government to remain in Constantinople where it would be more vulnerable to French pressure.

The end product of this Anglo-French compromise was a harsh and humiliating treaty. Constantinople remained Turkish, but Thrace and most of the European coastline of the Sea of Marmara and the Dardanelles were to go to Greece. In the Smyrna region the Greeks were also given responsibility for internal administration and defence, while an Armenian state was to be set up with access across Turkish territory to the Black Sea. The Straits were to be controlled by an international commission and an Allied financial committee was to have the right to inspect Turkey's finances. By a separate agreement zones were also awarded to France and Italy in southern Turkey.

To ensure the acceptance of the Treaty, an inter-Allied expedition occupied Constantinople in March 1920 and forced the Sultan to dismiss his Cabinet and declare Kemal a rebel. Inevitably this pushed Kemal into openly challenging the Treaty, thereby running the risk of a

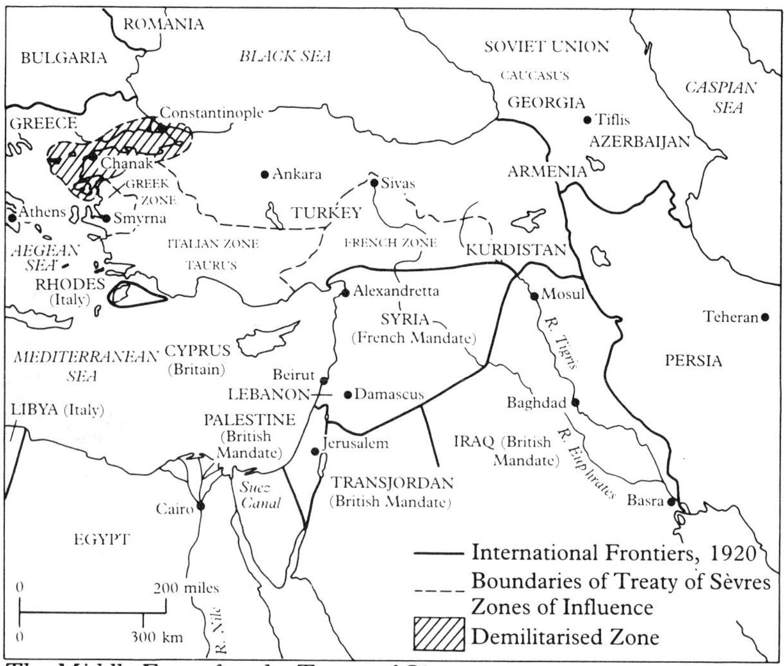

The Middle East after the Treaty of Sèvres

clash between the Kemalist and Allied forces. The French and Italians were unwilling to fight to enforce the Treaty but Lloyd George persuaded them to agree to allow Greek forces to advance from Smyrna and head off Kemal's threat to Constantinople. The initial success of the Greek army ensured that the Treaty was at last signed on 10 August, but only at the cost of escalating conflict with the Kemalists forces. Kemal was able to exploit Lenin's suspicions that the western powers were aiming to destroy Bolshevism, to undermine the Treaty of Sèvres. A joint Russo-Turkish attack destroyed Armenia in 1920, and the subsequent Treaty of March 1921, settling the Russo-Turkish frontier in the Caucasus, enabled Kemal to concentrate his forces against the Greeks without fear of Russian intervention from the north. By August 1922 he was poised to enter Constantinople and the Straits zone, which were still occupied by Allied troops. Both the Italians and French rapidly withdrew leaving the British isolated. As Churchill was later to write:

> 1 The catastrophe which Greek recklessness and Allied procrastination, division, and intrigue had long prepared now broke upon Europe. The signatories of the treaty of Sèvres had only been preserved in their world of illusion by the shield of Greece. That
> 5 shield was now shattered.

Kemal, however, avoided direct confrontation with the British forces and negotiated an armistice which gave him virtually all he wanted: the Greeks withdrew from eastern Thrace and Adrianople and the British recognised Turkish control over Constantinople and the Straits.

Although this incident, known as the Chanak crisis, contributed to Lloyd George's resignation, the abdication of the Sultan of Turkey and to a decisive diplomatic defeat for Britain, paradoxically the subsequent international conference of Lausanne, which met to revise the Treaty of Sèvres, resulted in an agreement in July 1923, that has been described by Professor Anderson as 'a victory for the western and above all for the British point of view'. Kemal, anxious not to be dependent on Russia agreed to the creation of small demilitarised zones on both sides of the Straits and the freedom of navigation through them for Britain, France, Italy and Japan. He also insisted on the abolition of foreign control over Turkish finances. This was a serious blow to the French hopes of re-establishing their pre-war influence over Turkish finances, and arguably they, apart from the Greeks, lost more than any other Power as a consequence of the new Treaty of Lausanne.

The Chanak crisis in no way affected the fate of Turkey's former Arab provinces. In February 1919, in deference to Wilson and the Fourteen Points, Britain and France agreed that they could only exercise power over these territories in the name of the League of Nations. It took several more months of bitter argument before the British agreed to a French mandate in Syria and also French access to the oil wells in Mosul and Iraq. The frontiers between the British mandates of Palestine and Iraq and the French mandate of Syria were then finalised in December.

7 The Russian Dimension

The success of the peace treaties depended directly in eastern Europe, and also to a great extent in the Near East, on Russian acceptance of the decisions taken at Paris. The outcome of the Russian civil war was therefore of crucial importance. In the fluid situation of 1919 both the western powers and Russia pursued parallel policies. The Bolsheviks tried to stir up revolution within central and western Europe, while at the same time establishing tentative diplomatic contacts with both the Germans and the Allies. They also tempted the Allied Powers with the prospect of renewing trade links and with talks on the possibility of repaying the former tsarist regime's international debts .

The Allies maintained a naval blockade, but they too also wanted to keep open diplomatic contacts with Lenin as an insurance in case the Bolsheviks were victorious in the civil war. In April, when the Whites were on the offensive and appeared to be winning the struggle, the Council of Four stepped up the dispatch of war material to them, although under pressure from Lloyd George and Wilson, who were anxious to avoid dangerously open ended military commitments, it also slowly began to evacuate the Allied troops sent to Russia in 1918 (see page 17). Only with the failure of the Whites in the winter of 1919-20 did the Allies raise the blockade and again give priority to the resumption of commercial and diplomatic contacts with Soviet Russia.

In early 1919 the Germans were not only aware that they might be able to improve the peace terms by impressing the Allies with their importance as a bulwark against Bolshevism, but that also the Bolsheviks might at some juncture be a potential ally against Britain and France. Like the Allies they therefore adopted an ambivalent policy towards Russia.

As long as the Russian civil war lasted, neither the future of the Baltic states nor Poland's eastern frontiers could be fixed. Latvia and Estonia had been occupied by the Bolsheviks in the winter of 1918-19. An alliance of White Russians, Swedish and Finnish volunteers and a brigade of German Free Corps (nationalist volunteers) troops liberated them, but although the Allies ordered their withdrawal, they did not immediately recognise the independence of the Baltic states. In the event of a White victory in Russia, these states would almost certainly have been swallowed up by Russia, as the French ideally wanted a strong non-Bolshevik Russia to help keep Germany in check. The independence of the Baltic states was only assured when Bolshevik Russia recognised them in 1920.

The Poles exploited the chaos in Russia to seize as much territory as they could. In December 1919 they rejected the proposed eastern frontier based on recommendations put forward by Lord Curzon, the British Foreign Minister, and in early 1920 embarked on a full-scale invasion of the Ukraine. By August Bolshevik forces had pushed the Poles back to Warsaw and the Germans were gleefully anticipating the collapse of the hated Polish state, and with it the whole of the Versailles settlement covering eastern Europe. However, with the help of French military supplies and advisers the Poles rallied and managed to inflict a decisive defeat on the Red Army just outside Warsaw. A military balance was thus created in eastern Europe, and in March 1921 Poland's eastern frontiers were at last fixed by the Treaty of Riga. Poland annexed a considerable area of Belorussia and the eastern Ukraine, all of which lay well to the east of the proposed Curzon line.

8 The Struggle to Enforce the Treaty of Versailles, 1920-3

The task of supervising the execution of the Treaty of Versailles was made infinitely more difficult by the refusal of the American Senate to ratify the Treaty of Versailles. Britain and France with some assistance from Italy and Belgium were left to implement a treaty which had been negotiated on the assumption of American participation.

Both powers had conflicting ideas of how best to ensure that Germany carried out the Treaty of Versailles. Essentially, Britain as the centre of a world-wide empire, wanted to see a balance of power in Europe that would prevent either French or German domination and leave her free to deal with the growing challenges to her power in India, Egypt and Ireland. She was convinced, too, that only a prosperous and peaceful Germany could pay reparations and play its part in Europe as one of the main engines of the European economy. For France the German problem was an over-riding priority. French policy oscillated uneasily between occasionally exploring the possibilities of economic co-operation with Germany, and more usually of applying coercive measures designed permanently to weaken Germany and to force her to fulfil the Treaty. Britain increasingly opposed any further weakening of Germany, but was also apprehensive about Franco-German economic co-operation which might lead to the creation of an economic community capable of discriminating against British trade. Essentially neither France nor Britain were strong enough to make their policies prevail. In the absence of help from America or of co-operation from a liberal and 'tamed' Germany both remained ultimately dependent on the Entente.

The overriding aim of German foreign policy was essentially to bring about by any practical means the revision of the Treaty of Versailles. There appeared in 1920 to be two obvious ways of achieving this: one was to exploit Anglo-French differences in the hope that these would weaken the Allies and lead to concessions to Germany; the other, favoured by von Seeckt, the chief of the German army, influential sections in the German Foreign Office and some industrialists was to come to an understanding with Russia which would enable Germany to oppose Britain and France more effectively. However, this last option was one which Berlin pursued with caution as it feared the spread of Communism.

For the first six months of 1920 Allied attempts to carry out the Treaty were met in Germany at every level by a mixture of outright defiance and a more subtle policy of procrastination. Lloyd George and Millerand hoped to break the deadlock by direct talks with the German leaders at the Spa Conference in July 1920. Grudging agreement to accelerate disarmament and to accept a new schedule of coal deliveries was only secured under the threat of an Allied occupation of the Ruhr. German proposals for reparation payments, however, still remained vague and imprecise.

Thus inevitably the problem of German reparation came to dominate European diplomacy. Lloyd George and Millerand hoped to solve the problem by fixing a global total as soon as possible on the assumption that once Germany knew the full sum of her debts she would be able to raise credit privately in America and begin payments. The French also explored the possibilities of some kind of economic co-operation with Germany. On 26 August 1920 the German Foreign Minister was informed that the French Minister of Finance:

> 1 ... was disposed to talk unofficially with the German Government
> about the application of the financial clauses of the Treaty of
> Versailles ... The French government would abandon a part of its
> treaty rights, if in exchange for this very great concession the
> 5 German government decides to give it satisfaction on other points.

A year later a Franco-German agreement was actually signed at Wiesbaden, which aimed to off-set the costs of German assistance with rebuilding the devastated regions of France against the reparation bill, but it ran into bitter opposition from both German and French industrialists, and was effectively abandoned.

At the end of April 1921 the Reparation Commission at last fixed a global total for reparations of 132 milliard gold marks. It was greeted with an explosion of rage in Germany and had to be imposed on Berlin by yet another threat to occupy the Ruhr. The response of the Germans to the Allied reparation demands had united Britain and France, but events in Upper Silesia in the summer of 1921 were soon to divide them. The plebiscite in Upper Silesia had produced an ambiguous result which re-opened the Anglo-French arguments over Poland. The British argued that its result justified keeping the key industrial region of the province German, thereby facilitating the payment of reparations, while the French insisted that it should be awarded to Poland, which desperately needed it to strengthen her industrial base. Then in May

1921 the Polish Upper Silesians revolted and seized control of the industrial area. The French refused to allow German troops to restore order and the Plebiscite Commission, the president of which was a French general, unofficially recognised the rebels' authority. Lloyd George, in a speech that reverberated through the capitals of Europe and caused a crisis in Anglo-French relations, pointedly argued that:

> 1 ... Either the Allies ought to insist upon the Treaty being respected, or they ought to allow the Germans to do it. Not merely to disarm Germany, but to say that such troops as she has got are not to be permitted to take part in restoring order in what, until the decision
> 5 comes, is their own province - that is not fair. Fair play is what England stands for, and I hope she will stand for it to the end.

Order was eventually restored by Allied troops in July, but the deadlock between France and Britain over the future of Upper Silesia was only broken by referring the whole question to the League of Nations in August. Eventually a judgement was given in October 1921 which handed over most of the industrial areas to Poland.

The French had won a significant victory in their struggle to enforce their interpretation of the Versailles Treaty on both Germany and Britain but in December the German government dropped a bombshell by announcing that as a consequence of escalating inflation it could not raise sufficient hard currency to meet the next instalment of reparation payments. This gave Lloyd George the opportunity to launch a major initiative. He was convinced that Germany needed a temporary moratorium, or postponement of reparation payments, to put her economy in order, while in the longer term the key to the payment of reparations and a European economic revival lay in setting up a European alliance of industrial nations, including Germany, to rebuild Russia. This, Lloyd George hoped, would generate a trade boom from the profits of which Germany would be able to pay reparations without damaging the commerce of the other European nations. Briand, the French Prime Minister, agreed to discuss these plans at Genoa in the spring at a conference to which the Russians would also be invited, but he could only win backing from the French Chamber for Lloyd George's radical plans, if they were coupled with a British military guarantee of French security. Britain's refusal to commit herself to more than a short-term pact led to the resignation of Briand and his replacement by the hard liner Raymond Poincaré in January 1922.

The Genoa Conference was a disaster. Poincaré's veto on any attempt to negotiate a moratorium on reparations heightened the Germans' suspicions of his policies and led to a separate Russo-German economic agreement. While the Germans were anxious to co-operate with Lloyd George, they responded to secret Russian diplomatic initiatives as an insurance against Poincaré. They feared particularly that

Poincaré might try to put extra pressure on Germany by using Article 116 of the Treaty of Versailles to encourage Russia to claim reparations (This article had originally been inserted to leave the door open to Russian claims in case the Whites won the civil war.) The Russians were suspicious of Lloyd George's proposed economic alliance, made up as it was of capitalist states, and preferred to continue their policy of dividing the capitalist powers by negotiating individual agreements with them. Thus both Russia and Germany signed a bilateral agreement at Rapallo during the conference renouncing their mutual war debts. Germany also agreed to confer with Moscow before joining any international consortium set up to exploit the Russian economy. Rapallo effectively killed Lloyd George's plan. It is hard not to see Rapallo as a miscalculation by the Germans. While it did something to re-establish Germany's diplomatic freedom of manoeuvre, it also intensified both French and British suspicions of her motives.

In July 1922 another major confrontation between France and Germany seemed inevitable when the German government requested a three year moratorium. At the same time Britain announced that, as America was demanding the repayment of British wartime debts, in turn she must insist on the repayment of an equivalent amount from her former allies.

To the French Britain's demand for these repayments contrasted painfully with the concessions Lloyd George was ready to offer the Germans. On 27 November the Poincaré cabinet decided finally that the occupation of the Ruhr was the only means of forcing Germany to pay reparations, and on 11 January French and Belgian troops moved into the Ruhr. Significantly Britain did not join in but adopted a policy of 'benevolent neutrality' towards France. For nine months the French occupation of the Ruhr was met by passive resistance and strikes which were financed by the German government. This increased the cost of the occupation, but it also triggered hyper-inflation in Germany. In September Germany was on the brink of collapse and the new Chancellor, Gustav Stresemann, called off passive resistance.

France, too, had exhausted herself and seriously weakened the franc in the prolonged Ruhr crisis. Her attempts to back Rhineland Separatism and to create an independent Rhineland currency were unsuccessful. In the Palatinate the Separatist leaders were assassinated by German nationalist agents from unoccupied Germany or lynched by angry crowds. Poincaré had thus little option but to co-operate with an Anglo-American initiative, for setting up a commission chaired by the American financier Charles G. Dawes. Its two committees of experts, one to study Germany's capacity for payment, and the other to advise on how she could best balance her budget and restore her currency, began work in early 1924.

As one French official accurately observed, the time was now past for dealing with Germany as 'victor to vanquished'. The Ruhr crisis marked the end of the attempts to carry out the Treaty of Versailles by force and the beginning of the gradual revision of the Treaty itself.

9 A Critical Assessment

The peace treaties of 1919-20 were seen by some contemporaries as a triumph of democracy, the rule of law, self determination and collective security against militarism, and by others as a hypocritical act of vengeance and economic ignorance. The treaties contained a unique combination of idealism and morality with old fashioned power politics. At past peace conferences there had been the assumption by both victors and the defeated that eventually the territorial settlement would be modified in a new war. In the Great War the slaughter had been so terrible that public opinion in Europe wanted future conflict prevented, whether by a draconian peace permanently weakening the Central Powers or by more liberal measures overseen by the League of Nations. Consequently the treaties of 1919-20 were judged by almost impossibly high standards.

Increasingly, as a result of Keynes' devastating criticisms in *The Economic Consequences of the Peace,* public opinion in Britain and America began to turn against Versailles. Keynes summarised his arguments as follows:

> 1 1 ... the treaty ignores the economic solidarity of Europe and by aiming at the destruction of the economic life of Germany it threatens the health and prosperity of the Allies themselves.
> 2 ... the German economic system as it existed before depended on
> 5 ... I. Overseas commerce as represented by her mercantile marine [most of which had to be handed over to the Allies], her colonies, her foreign investments, her exports... II. The exploitation of her coal and iron and the industries built upon them. ... The Treaty aims at the systematic destruction of [this system].

To the Germans Keynes' arguments seemed to provide the final proof that the Allies led by Clemenceau were out to destroy their country, yet viewed from the perspective of 1945 the Treaty of Versailles does not appear as harsh as it did in 1919. Germany was still potentially a Great Power. It is arguable too, that it was as much the hostility of the German industrialists and the refusal of the American Government to assist France financially as the rapacity of the Allies that rendered the payment of reparations so difficult to achieve. Most treaties are compromises, and even after their signature, Powers attempt to revise the clauses they dislike. It is quite possible to argue that the majority of the territorial clauses of the treaties signed in 1919-20 did represent a genuine compromise between Allied aims and the Fourteen Points. In defending the Treaties of Trianon and St. Germain, Churchill argued, for instance, that 'all the disputable areas put together were but a minute fraction of the whole. They were but exceptions which proved the rule'.

Unlike the Vienna settlement the peace treaties failed to create a new balance of power in Europe. The Habsburg Empire was replaced by a mosaic of small unstable states. Italy, despite the destruction of her historic enemy, Austria, felt cheated by the Peace and was to remain a revisionist power in the Mediterranean and the Adriatic. Even Britain and France, who gained most from Versailles, in fact secured only short-term advantages as they were too divided by mutual suspicions to implement the treaties in the crucial post war years.

Essentially the real weakness of the settlements of 1919-20 was that America, which had played such a part in negotiating them, was prevented by the vote in the Senate from helping to execute them. One American historian, Paul Birdsall, argued that:

> 1 the defection of the United States destroyed the Anglo-American preponderance which above all could have stabilised Europe. It impaired the authority and prestige of the League at its birth and it precipitated an Anglo-French duel which reduced Europe to the
> 5 chaos from which Hitler emerged to produce new chaos. ...

While it is debatable whether the American Senate can be held responsible for the rise of Hitler and the Second World War, there is no doubt that America's active presence in the Supreme Council of the Allies between 1920-3 and her participation in a military guarantee of France's frontiers would have had a decisive influence on European stabilisation in the immediate post-war years.

Making notes on the 'The Peace Settlements and the New Europe, 1919-23'

Your notes on this chapter should be fairly detailed, since the peace settlements are a favourite topic with the examiners. As you write them out you should always bear in mind these three key questions: 1) What were the aims of the peace makers? 2) To what extent were the treaties a compromise between conflicting aims? 3) How successful were the treaties up to 1923? (After you have read chapters 4, 5 and 6 you will be able to extend this date up to 1930 or 1939.) The following headings and sub-headings should provide you with an appropriate framework for your notes:

1 What were the problems facing the peacemakers?
2 The aims of the victorious Powers
2.1 American
2.2 French
2.3 British
2.4 Japanese and Italian

The Peace Settlements, 1919-23

Problems

1 Revolutionary condition of Europe
2 Russian civil war
3 Diverging Allied aims
4 Competing nationalisms
5 Desire for revenge
6 Hunger, disease, economic chaos
7 Allied lack of military strength

Principles

1 Independence for subject nations
2 International rule of law through the League of Nations
3 Disarmament and reparation from defeated powers
4 Determination to prove German war guilt
5 Selective (?) application of 14 points

The Versailles Settlement, June 1919

Territorial changes	Reparations	Disarmament	League of Nations
Independent Poland	Reparation Commission fixes amount of 132 milliard gold marks in May 1921	Abolition of conscription	Collective security
Plebiscites in U. Silesia, Schleswig and West Prussia	Prolonged struggle to force Germany to pay, 1921-3	Regular German army of 100,000	New principle of mandates
Alsace-Lorraine to France	France occupies Ruhr in Jan 1923	Very small fleet	Weakened by absence of USA
Saar administered by League of Nations	Dawes Commission Jan 1924	Allied control commissions in Germany until 1927	Germany and defeated powers initially excluded
Germany loses colonies and foreign investments		Rhineland occupied for 15 years	

The Eastern European, Balkan and Near East peace settlements

St Germain	Trianon	Neuilly	Sèvres	Riga
Czechoslovakia set up	Hungary loses 2/3 of her pre-war territory to Austria, Czechoslovakia and Romania	Bulgaria loses territory to Greece, Romania and Yugoslavia	Turks cede Middle East empire; Greeks gain Thrace; Straits controlled by Allies	Russia defeated by Poland, August 1920
Slovenia, Bosnia, Dalmatia to Yugoslavia			Revised at Lausanne, 1923: Greeks expelled, Constantinople back to Turkey	Poland's eastern frontiers fixed by Treaty of Riga, March 1921
Istria, Trieste and S. Tyrol to Italy				
Galicia to Poland				
Austria not to integrate with Germany				

Summary - The Peace Settlements and the New Europe, 1919-23

3 How was the Peace Conference organised?
4 The Settlement with Germany (Treaty of Versailles)
4.1 Reparations
4.2 Disarmament
4.3 Territorial settlement
4.4 Disposal of her colonies
4.5 The German reaction
5 The other treaties
5.1 St Germain
5.2 Trianon
5.3 Neuilly
5.4 Italian claims in the Adriatic
5.5 Sèvres: why it had to be renegotiated at Lausanne
6 Russia and the eastern European settlement.
7 The enforcement of Versailles, 1920-3
7.1 The reparation problem
7.2 Diverging Anglo-French policies
7.3 The Ruhr crisis
7.4 Why did the treaties fail?

Answering essay questions on *'The Peace Settlements and the New Europe, 1919-23'*

Questions on the peace settlements of 1919-23 are very popular with the examiners and regularly appear in both general outline papers and in the more specific papers covering a shorter time-span, such as the years 1917-39. Questions usually fall into two main groups: the more detailed questions requiring a critical analysis of the contents of the actual treaties and then those that are more concerned with the longer-term consequences of the treaties. In this last category examiners often expect you to trace the impact of the treaties up to 1930 or even 1939. Thus a discussion of this type of question is best left until you have read and noted the next chapter. Study the following titles which are all specific questions on the treaties.

1. 'Neither a peace of revenge nor a peace of reconciliation.' Was this the fatal weakness in the Treaty of Versailles?
2. Discuss the view that the Versailles settlement was an unsatisfactory compromise between hopes for reconciliation and a desire to punish Germany.
3. 'Vicious and short-sighted'. How correct is this assessment of the peace settlements of 1919-20?
4. Were the post-war treaties a defeat for Wilsonian liberalism?

Only one of these - number 4 - is set in the form of a simple question. In the others the examiner employs a popular technique, which we have already noticed, of putting forward an interpretation and asking you to assess it. You must be careful when answering this type of question not to fall into the trap of giving a long narrative account of the contents of the Treaty. You do not of course have to agree with the examiner. You will, as always, need to be analytical in your approach and to show, for instance in questions 1 and 2 , that almost every section of Versailles was in fact a compromise between the conflicting demands of the Allies and America. You should ask yourself whether this was necessarily a 'fatal weakness' in the Treaty. After all, diplomacy cannot usually succeed without compromise. Perhaps the refusal of America to ratify the Treaty was the real undoing of Versailles?

The next two questions are more general and require you to consider *all* the peace settlements. Clearly you must again avoid both excessive narrative and too much detail if you wish to finish the question in time! The best way to avoid this is to answer the questions thematically. For instance you could consider the treatment of the nationality problem by all the treaties in one section of the essay and then go on and analyse the military, economic, imperialist or annexationist aims in other sections. In question 4 you would also need to understand the implications of the Fourteen Points as well as knowing the details of Wilsonian diplomacy in Paris. As historical issues are so often complex and contradictory, you may well wish to question whether such statements as 'vicious and short-sighted' can be applied to all aspects of the peace treaties.

Source-based questions on *'The Peace Settlements and the New Europe, 1919-23'*

1 Clemenceau's Aims

Read carefully the extract from Clemenceau's speech on pages 28-9. Answer the following questions:

a) Who are the 'very high authorities' (line 5)? (2 marks)
b) What does Clemenceau mean by the 'balance ... spontaneously produced during the war' (lines 5-6)? (3 marks)
c) How useful is this extract as a guide to French policy at the Paris Peace Conference? (10 marks)

2 The German War Guilt Question

Read carefully the extracts from Wilson's speech at Omaha on page 27, Article 231 of the Treaty of Versailles on page 32 and the Berlin government's declaration in June on page 38. Also look at the cartoon on page 37. Answer the following questions:

a) Explain the meaning of 'Surrendering to force ... without retracting its opinion' (page 38 lines 1-2). (2 marks)
b) How do the extracts on pages 27 and 32 seek to emphasise

Germany's war guilt? Why was this so important for the Allies and America? (6 marks)

c) How effectively does the cartoon contradict the declaration by the German government? (7 marks)

3 The Peace Settlements in the Balkans and the Near East

Read carefully the comments by Professor Macartney and Winston Churchill on pages 40 and 43.

a) What does Macartney mean by 'no frontier could be drawn, which does not leave national minorities on at least one side of it'? (lines 9-11). Give one example which illustrates this point. (4 marks)
b) What does 'the shield of Greece' mean? (page 43, line 4) (3 marks)
c) How useful to a historian of the peace settlements in the Balkans and the Near East are these two extracts? (8 marks)

4 British policy towards Germany, 1920-3

Read carefully the extract from Keynes' arguments on page 49 and Lloyd George's speech of May 1921 on page 47.

a) Why according to Keynes did the Treaty threaten the 'health and prosperity of the Allies' (line 3)? (2 marks)
b) What did Lloyd George mean by: 'Either the Allies ought to insist upon the Treaty being respected or they ought to allow the Germans to do it' (page 47 lines 1-2)? (3 marks)
c) In what way do these extracts help you to understand Britain's policy towards Germany, 1920-3? (10 marks)

CHAPTER 4

The Politics of Reconciliation, 1924-30

1 Introduction

The agreement to implement the Dawes Plan and the signature of the Locarno Agreements together mark a fresh start after the bitterness of the immediate post-war years. For the first time since 1914 Germany and the 'ex-Allies' (Britain, France and Italy) met in August 1924 as equals in London and negotiated a revised payments schedule for reparations (the Dawes Plan). Then a year later at Locarno, in Switzerland, they signed a security pact guaranteeing Germany's existing frontiers with France and Belgium.

For the next four years the pace of international co-operation quickened and the League of Nations, despite a hesitant start, grew in authority and influence. After Germany joined the League in 1926 a new framework for Great Power co-operation evolved. The Foreign Ministers of Britain, France and Germany (Austen Chamberlain, Aristide Briand and Gustav Stresemann) regularly attended the meetings of the League Council and Assembly and played a key part in directing their business. The partnership of these three statesmen came to symbolise the new era of peace and apparent stabilisation. Stresemann was actually awarded the Nobel Peace Prize in 1926 for his part in the Locarno negotiations. Were these men really the great peacemakers they seemed or were they pursuing the same aims as their predecessors, although somewhat more subtly? Some historians, like Peter Krüger, who has written on the foreign policy of the Weimar republic, argue that Stresemann's foreign policy anticipated the essentially peaceful aims of the German *Bundesrepublik* between 1949 and 1990, while other historians, particularly those writing in the immediate aftermath of 1945, see Stresemann as a link in the chain connecting Bismarck with Hitler. Certainly up to 1920 Stresemann had been an uncompromising German nationalist, but in 1923 the gravity of the Ruhr crisis did convince him that only through compromise could Germany survive, achieve the revision of Versailles and the re-establishment of her power in Europe. His hatred of Versailles was as strong as any other German's. Neither had Briand, who had threatened Germany with the occupation of the Ruhr in April 1921 (see page 46), really changed his fundamental aims. He still sought security against German aggression, but after the failure of Poincaré's Ruhr policy, he was determined to achieve it by co-operation with Britain and Germany herself. In many ways Briand was the right man for the moment. He had a genius for compromise, or as one French historian, Professor Néré has observed, 'for creating the half-light conducive to harmony'. Chamberlain, too, pursued the same policies as his predecessors, but he had a much stronger hand to play. As a consequence of France's failure in the Ruhr, America's refusal to play a political role in Europe and Soviet Russia's isolation, the Dawes Plan and the Locarno Treaties made Britain the virtual arbiter between France and Germany. In that enviable but temporary position Chamberlain could simultaneously counsel restraint and patience to the Germans, compromise to the French, whilst retaining the maximum of freedom for Britain to attend to the pressing problems of her empire.

After the traumas of the Depression and the Second World War the Locarno era appears in retrospect to be a brief but doomed era of hope and international progress. Most studies of this period stress the fragility and inadequacy of the stabilisation policies pursued by America and the Great European Powers and argue that their failure was inevitable. However, an important exception to this view is C.S. Maier's thesis in *Recasting Bourgeois Europe* that the European politicians of the late 1920s did in fact produce a viable model of stability. He argues with hindsight that 'the Depression, National Socialism and the Second World War were interruptions, albeit catastrophic ones, between a provisional political and social settlement [after Locarno] and a more permanent one [after 1945]'.

2 The Dawes Plan and the Locarno Agreements, 1924-5

The Dawes Plan played a crucial part in ending the bitter conflict over reparations which had nearly escalated into open war during the Ruhr occupation. It was welcomed enthusiastically in April 1924 by the British Treasury as

> ... the only constructive suggestion for escape from the present position, which if left must inevitably lead to war, open or concealed between Germany and France.

However, like all international compromises, some Powers had to compromise rather more than others. Although it did not alter the overall reparation total which had been fixed in 1921, it did recommend an 800 million gold mark loan, which was to be raised mainly in America, to assist the restoration of the German economy. This was a crucially important component of the plan because it opened the way for American investment in Germany. Annual reparations payments were to start gradually and rise at the end of five years to their maximum level. These payments were to be guaranteed by the revenues of the German railways and of several key industries. A committee of foreign experts sitting in Berlin under the chairmanship of an American official was to ensure that the actual payments were transferred to the ex-Allies in such a way that the German economy was not damaged. The Plan was provisional and was to be re-negotiated over the next ten years.

There was much that the French disliked about the plan. For instance it was not clear to them how the Germans could be compelled to pay if they again defaulted as they did in 1922. So they initially attempted to make their acceptance dependent on concessions from London and Washington on inter-allied debts and on the negotiation of a new security pact with Britain. The Americans threatened to withdraw from the Dawes Commission in the event of French non-acceptance, while Ramsay MacDonald, the new Labour British Prime Minister, vaguely promised to make a 'full exploration of the whole question of security' once the Dawes Plan was implemented. With the defeat of Poincaré in the elections of June 1924 French willingness to co-operate markedly increased. Essentially, if the French were ever to receive any reparation payments and to avoid isolation they had little option but to go along with the Dawes Plan.

The Germans also disliked the Plan as it placed their railways and some of their industry ultimately under international control and did nothing about scaling down their reparation debts. Stresemann who, after the fall of his cabinet in November 1923, was now Foreign Minister, realised, however, that Germany also had no alternative but to accept the Plan if the French were to be persuaded to evacuate the Ruhr sooner rather than later. Agreement to implement the Dawes Plan and to withdraw French and Belgian forces from the Ruhr within twelve months was achieved at the London Conference in August 1924. The new balance of power in Europe was clearly revealed when Britain and America devised a formula for effectively blocking France's ability to act alone against Germany in the event of another default in reparation payments. If Germany again refused to pay, it was agreed that Britain as a member of the Reparation Commission would have the right to appeal to the International Court at the Hague and an American representative would immediately join the Reparation Commission. Joint Anglo-American pressure would then be more than enough to constrain France from reoccupying the Ruhr. Deprived of much of their influence on the Reparation Commission, the French had undoubtedly suffered a major diplomatic defeat at the London Conference.

The Dawes Plan by bringing the Ruhr Crisis to an end had, together with the German measures to stabilise the mark, made Germany an attractive prospect for American investment. To a certain extent one of the pre-conditions for a European economic recovery was now in place, but investment was to come from individuals and banks and was not guaranteed by the American government nor was it accompanied by offers of military security to the French. Thus should a new economic crisis blow up, American money could melt away and France could be left facing a strong and aggressive Germany. The French were therefore determined to plug this security gap. Initially the French looked to the League of Nations where the Draft Treaty of Mutual Assistance or Geneva Protocol had been drawn up. This sought to provide world-wide security by obliging members of the League to come to the assistance of any state which was a victim of aggression and which was situated in the same continent as themselves. By the time the British Labour Government was defeated in the election of October 1924 it was clear that no British Government with an empire spread all over the world could really agree to become a world policeman on the scale required by the Geneva Protocol, and it was finally vetoed by Austen Chamberlain in March 1925.

The French had little option but to continue to insist, in as far as they still could, on the literal implementation of the Treaty of Versailles. They refused to agree to the evacuation of the Cologne Zone, which was due in January 1925 (see page 35), on the grounds that Germany had not yet carried out the military clauses of the Treaty 'either in the spirit or in the letter'. The urgent need to reassure the French of Germany's pacific intentions, and so secure the evacuation of Cologne, prompted Stresemann, on the unofficial advice of Lord D'Abernon, the British Ambassador in Berlin, to put forward a complex scheme for an international guarantee by the European Great Powers of the Rhineland and of the status quo in western Europe.

Chamberlain at first suspected the proposals of being an attempt to divide France and Britain, but he rapidly grasped that it was potentially a marvellous opportunity to square the circle by achieving both French security and the evacuation of Cologne without committing Britain to a military pact with France, which, as Chamberlain knew, the Cabinet would never tolerate. Briand was aware that only within the framework of an international agreement on the lines put forward by Stresemann could he in any way formally commit Britain to coming to the assistance of France.

In the ensuing negotiations Briand successfully persuaded Chamberlain and Stresemann to widen the international guarantee to cover the Belgo-German frontier. He also attempted to extend it to Germany's eastern frontiers, but this was rejected both by Stresemann and Chamberlain. However, Stresemann did offer arbitration agreements to Poland and Czechoslovakia, although he refused to recognise their frontiers with Germany as permanent. Chamberlain was quite specific that it was in British interests only to guarantee the status quo in western Europe. He told the House of Commons in November 1925:

> 1 A form of guarantee which is so general that we undertake exactly the same obligations in defence, shall I say of the Polish Corridor (for which no British Government ever will or ever can risk the bones of a British grenadier) as we extend to these international
> 5 arrangements or conditions on which, as our History shows, our national existence depends, is a guarantee so wide and general that it carries no conviction whatever and gives no sense of security to those who are concerned in our action.

Even in western Europe Chamberlain was anxious to narrow the scope for British intervention. He assured the Cabinet that Britain would not go to war over 'some trifling infringement' of the agreement by Germany.

The negotiations were completed at the Locarno Conference, 5-16 October 1925. The Locarno Agreements consisted of four arbitration treaties, signed by Germany with France, Belgium, Poland and Czechoslovakia, and of a Treaty of Mutual Guarantee, by which, Belgium, Britain, France, Germany and Italy were bound to uphold the demilitarisation of the Rhineland and the existing frontiers between Belgium and Germany and France and Germany. Italy had no direct interest in the Rhineland but was brought into the guarantee largely because France hoped she might act as a counter weight to Britain's tendency to appease the Germans. Belgium, France and Germany also pledged themselves not to attack each other unless in self-defence. If a relatively minor incident on one of the frontiers covered by Locarno occurred, the injured party (for example France) would first appeal to the Council of the League of Nations, and if the complaint was upheld, the guarantors would assist the injured state to secure compensation from the aggressor (for example Germany). In the event of a serious violation of the treaty the guarantors would act immediately, although they would still eventually refer the issue to the Council.

Throughout most of western Europe and America the Locarno Treaties were greeted with what one diplomat, Harold Nicolson, called an 'orgiastic gush'. It appeared as if real peace had at last come. Had France now achieved the security she had for so long been seeking? Of all the Great Powers the French gained least from Locarno. Briand certainly intended that it should mark a final German acceptance of the Versailles system and that this would be further strengthened by a British guarantee. It is true that France's eastern frontier was now secure, but under Locarno she could no longer threaten the Ruhr to bring pressure to bear on Berlin in the event of a war between her main eastern European ally, Poland, and Germany. The British had managed to give France the illusion of security, but the provision for referring all but major violations of the Locarno Agreements to the League before taking action ensured that the British government would in practice be able to determine through its own representative on the Council what action, if any, it should take. For Britain there were two main advantages to Locarno: it tied France down and prevented her from repeating the Ruhr occupation. Also by improving relations between Germany and the Western Powers and by holding out the prospect of German membership of the League, it discouraged any close co-operation between Moscow and Berlin.

Locarno was deeply unpopular with the German nationalists, but for Stresemann it was the key to the gradual process of revising the Treaty. He wrote to the German ex-Crown Prince on 7 September 1925:

After Locarno, Punch *cartoon, 28 October 1925*

> 1 ... there are three great tasks that confront German foreign policy in the more immediate future. In the first place the solution of the Reparation question in a sense tolerable for Germany, and the assurance of peace, which is essential for the recovery of our 5 strength.
> Secondly the protection of the Germans abroad, those 10 to 12 millions of our kindred who now live under a foreign yoke in foreign lands. The third great task is the readjustment of our Eastern frontiers: the recovery of Danzig, the Polish frontier, and a 10 correction of the frontier of Upper Silesia.

By assuring Germany of peace in the west, and by not placing her eastern frontiers with Poland under international guarantee, Locarno left open the eventual possibility of revision.

Stresemann's aims were therefore diametrically opposed to Briand's, but both desired peace and therein lay the real importance of Locarno. It was a symbol of a new age of reconciliation and co-operation. Locarno was, as Professor Néré has observed, 'an eminently diplomatic piece of work, which consisted of postponing the problems and relying on time to solve them'.

3 The 'Locarno Spirit' and the Re-emergence of Germany as a Great Power

The 'Locarno Spirit' was an elusive concept which was interpreted differently in London, Paris and Berlin. All three Powers agreed that it involved good will and concessions, yet the scope and timing of these concessions were a matter of constant and often acrimonious debate. Both Stresemann and Briand had to convince their countrymen that the Locarno policy was working. Briand had to show that he was not giving too much away, while Stresemann had to satisfy German public opinion that his policy of fulfilment was resulting in real concessions from the ex-Allies. It can be argued that not only the survival of Stresemann's policy but of the German Republic itself depended on ever more ambitious diplomatic successes. What would happen once these were unobtainable?

The atmosphere of detente created by Locarno quickly led to the evacuation of the Cologne Zone in January 1926. As soon as the last troops departed, the Germans and many in the British Labour and Liberal parties claimed that the occupation of the remaining two Rhineland zones was increasingly an anachronism. In October 1926 Germany at last joined the League of Nations and received a permanent seat on the Council.

Stresemann exploited every opportunity both inside and outside the League to accelerate the revision of Versailles. One initiative in particular illustrates both the new informal approach to international politics during the Locarno era and the growing friendship between Stresemann and Briand. Over a gourmet meal in the village of Thoiry in France near the Swiss frontier, Stresemann outlined to Briand a fantastic scheme for bribing the French with a loan raised in America to evacuate the Rhineland and to return the Saar and its mines to Germany. Initially Briand showed considerable interest, but when it became clear that the Americans were not ready to subscribe to another loan and that by December, contrary to all expectations, the French Treasury had stabilised the franc, the deal was quietly shelved. Undaunted Stresemann continued to wrest piecemeal concessions from the ex-Allies. In January 1927 the Allied Disarmament Commission was withdrawn from Germany, and in the following August Britain, France and Belgium withdrew a further 10,000 troops from their garrisons in the Rhineland.

In 1928 the German Government launched at Geneva a major initiative to persuade Britain and France to evacuate the Rhineland and, together with America, to agree to a revision of the Dawes Plan. The Germans stressed that the Plan had originally only been accepted as an interim solution. The American bankers were ready to contemplate a revised reparations settlement as it was obvious that once the German Government had to pay the full annual instalments under the Dawes Plan, it would lack sufficient foreign exchange to meet the interest on the loans raised since 1924 in the United States. The French were ready to accept in principle a comprehensive international debt and reparations settlement and even the evacuation of the last two zones in the Rhineland, but Briand was determined to link this with setting up a new international body to ensure that the Rhineland remained demilitarised after evacuation. The whole question of reparations was considered throughout the winter of 1928-9 by another committee of experts chaired by the American banker, Owen Young. The tough negotiating position of the German experts, who demanded the restoration of the Polish Corridor and Upper Silesia, reflected the new more nationalist mood of German politics where the leadership of both the Nationalist and the Catholic Centre Parties had shifted further rightwards. The Young Committee announced its recommendations in June 1929: the overall reparation sum was reduced from 132 milliard (gold) marks to 40 milliard (gold) marks and would be paid over the course of 59 years. The international controls over the German economy set up under the Dawes Plan would be dismantled and the Reparation Commission would no longer be able to initiate sanctions.

The implementation of the Young Plan and the Rhineland question were discussed at the Hague Conference in August 1929. Initially Britain and France clashed bitterly over their share of reparations. The new Labour Chancellor of the Exchequer, Snowden, was determined to demand compensation for the £200 million war debt payments the British Treasury had already made to the Americans, but eventually after a dramatic midnight confrontation, he agreed to accept only 75 per cent of his original demands. Over the Rhineland it was the French who dug in their heals in a last desperate attempt to extract concessions. It was only when Stresemann threatened not to sign the reparation agreement that Briand was forced to agree to its evacuation by 30 June 1930. His plans for setting up a Commission of Verification and Conciliation to monitor demilitarisation had to be abandoned under joint Anglo-German pressure. The British feared that, far from conciliating, it would in fact exacerbate differences between Germany and the ex-Allies.

The agreement to end the Rhineland occupation certainly helped make the Young Plan acceptable in Germany, where in December the government had to face a referendum forced upon them by the Nazi and Nationalist parties declaring that its signature would be an act of high treason. This was easily defeated and the Young Plan was officially implemented on 20 January.

With the evacuation of the Rhineland, Germany's restoration to Great Power status was virtually complete. Briand, like his successors in the 1950s, appears to have come to the conclusion that Germany could only be peacefully contained through some form of European federation. At the tenth Assembly of the League of Nations in 1929, Briand outlined an ambitious, but vague scheme:

> 1 I believe that there should be some kind of federal link between peoples who are grouped together geographically, like the peoples of Europe. These peoples should be able to come into contact at any time, to discuss their common interests, and to make a joint
> 5 resolution. In a word, they should establish between them a tie of solidarity which will enable them, at the desired moment, to face up to serious circumstances, should they arise ... Obviously the association will function most of all in the economic field: this is the most immediate necessity. I believe that in this field we can
> 10 succeed. I am also sure, however, that from the political or social point of view, the federal link could be beneficial, without interfering with the sovereignty of any of the nations which might form part of an association of this kind.

Stresemann reacted favourably and urged both a European customs union and a common currency. Briand was then entrusted by the 27 European members of the League with the task of formulating his plan more precisely, but when it was circulated to the chancelleries of Europe in May 1930, the whole economic and political climate of Europe had dramatically changed. Stresemann had died and the political crisis in Germany caused by the onset of the Depression brought to power a government under Heinrich Brüning that was more interested in a customs union with Austria than in a European federation. The German

Cabinet finally rejected the memorandum on 8 July 1930. A week later it was also rejected by Britain on the grounds

> that an exclusive and independent European Union of the kind proposed might emphasise or create tendencies to inter-continental rivalries and hostilities which it is important in the general interest to diminish and to avoid.

It is tempting to argue that this most dramatic manifestation of the Locarno spirit, which was killed off by the economic crisis that was eventually to bring Hitler to power, was one of the lost opportunities of History. On the other hand, it would be a mistake to view it through the eyes of a late-twentieth century European federalist. Essentially Stresemann hoped that it would open the door to an accelerated revision of the Treaty of Versailles, while Briand calculated that it would have the opposite effect. Perhaps under favourable circumstances it could at least have provided a framework within which Franco-German differences could have been solved, but would the French at that date have been ready to alienate Britain and seek a close partnership with Germany?

4 Russia and Eastern Europe

The Dawes Plan and the Locarno Treaties temporarily stabilised western Europe and Germany. Soviet Russia with her immense potential power remained on the fringes of Europe still looking towards Germany as a possible ally against the Versailles Powers, while the eastern European and Balkan states remained weak and volatile.

a) Russia

The Soviet Government, which after the death of Lenin in January 1924 increasingly fell under the control of Stalin, viewed the progress made in stabilising western Europe through the Dawes Plan and the Locarno Agreements with both dismay and hostility, as it feared that this would strengthen the anti-Bolshevik forces in Europe and delay revolution in Germany. The Russians initially attempted to deflect Stresemann from his Locarno policy, first with the offer of a military alliance against Poland, and then when that did not work, with the contradictory threat of joining with France to guarantee Poland's western frontiers. Stresemann, aware of Russia's attempts to stir up revolution in Germany in 1923, was not ready to abandon the Locarno policy, but he was anxious to keep open his links with Moscow and consolidate the Rapallo Agreement of 1922 (see page 48) if only as a possible insurance against Anglo-French pressure in the west. Thus the Russians were able first to negotiate a commercial treaty with Germany in October 1925. Then in April 1926 at a time when the Poles and the French were trying to delay Germany's membership of the League Council, they were able to persuade Stresemann to sign the Berlin Treaty. Essentially this was a neutrality pact confirming Rapallo, in which both powers agreed to remain neutral if either party was attacked by a third power.

Relations between Russia and Britain sharply deteriorated when the returning Conservative Government refused in October 1924 to ratify the Anglo-Soviet General Treaty which had been negotiated by the outgoing Labour administration. In 1927, after ordering a raid on the offices of the official Soviet trading company, Arcos, in an attempt to discover evidence of espionage, the British Government severed all official relations with Russia. Only in 1929 with the return of Labour were ambassadors again exchanged. This outbreak of the first 'Anglo-Soviet cold war', as the American historian, Jacobson, has called it, strengthened Stalin's instinctive siege mentality towards the West. Increasingly the main thrust of Soviet foreign policy in the late Twenties was to exploit anti-western feeling in the Middle East, China and India.

b) Poland and the Balkans

With the victory of the Bolsheviks in the Russian Civil War, the French began to build up a series of alliances in eastern Europe to take the place of their original pre-war alliance with Tsarist Russia. In March 1921 they concluded an alliance with Poland which, because it was hated by Russia and Germany and was on bad terms with Czechoslovakia and Lithuania, was the most vulnerable of the east European states. The country was dependent on the maintenance of the Treaty of Versailles for its very existence.

The French were less successful in organising the other new states created at Versailles into a defensive alliance against Germany. In August 1920 Czechoslovakia and Yugoslavia signed a pact which became known as the Little Entente, and were joined by Romania in 1921. However, it was primarily directed against Hungary and was designed to prevent the return of the Habsburgs and the revision of the Trianon Treaty. Only in 1924 did Paris succeed in concluding a treaty with Czechoslovakia but, again, it was not strictly an anti-German pact. It would only come into operation in the event of a restoration of the royal families of Austria or Germany or of an Austrian *Anschluss* (union) with Germany. Despite attempts by Italy to challenge French influence in the Balkans, the French government was able to capitalise on the unease caused by the way in which Italy exploited the role of protector of Albania given to her by the Conference of Ambassadors (see page 72), to sign a treaty with Romania guaranteeing her frontiers (1926) and a treaty of friendship with Yugoslavia (1927). By the end of the decade French influence was preponderant in the Balkans.

5 The League of Nations

The League was a part of the international settlements negotiated in 1919-20. Inevitably the tensions and divisions inherent in these were also present in the League. The absence in 1920 of three Great Powers from the League reflected the reality of the international situation where both Germany and the USSR licked their wounds in defensive isolation, while the American Government, after having played such a key role in negotiating the new peace settlement, had been forced by Congress to disengage from most of its international responsibilities. The League's ultimate success or failure was dependent on the progress made by the Great Powers in stabilising Europe after the First World War. Not surprisingly the League's golden age coincided with the new stability created by the Locarno era.

a) Its Constitution

In retrospect it is possible to argue that the League's constitution provided too many loop holes for war, supported the status quo which favoured the Great Powers and in the final analysis lacked the machinery for collective action against an aggressor. Yet even if it had a theoretically perfect constitution, would its history have been any different? Was the official British commentary on the Covenant not realistic when it pointed out:

> 1 if the nations of the future are in the main selfish, grasping and warlike, no instrument or machinery will restrain them. It is only possible to establish an organisation which may make peaceful co-operation easy and hence customary, and to trust in the
> 5 influence of custom to mould opinion.

The initial members of the League were the 32 Allied states which had signed the peace treaties and 12 neutral states. By 1926 all the ex-enemy states including Germany had joined, but Soviet Russia did not do so until 1934, and America never did. The League at first consisted of three main organs: the Assembly, the Council and the Secretariat. The Assembly was essentially a deliberative chamber where each state, regardless of its size, was allotted three representatives. It was a jealously guarded principle that even the smallest state had the right to be heard on international issues. The Council in 1920 had four permanent members, Britain, France, Italy and Japan. In 1926 this was increased by one when Germany joined. The smaller states were represented by a changing rota of four temporary members,later increased to seven, who were all selected by the Assembly. As the Council met more frequently than the Assembly and was dominated by the Great Powers, it gradually developed as an executive committee or 'cabinet' of the Assembly, and worked out the details and implementation of policies which the Assembly had endorsed in principle. Decisions in both bodies were normally taken by unanimous vote. The votes of states involved in a dispute under discussion by the League were discounted when the Assembly and Council voted on recommendations for its settlement. In this way they could be prevented from vetoing an otherwise unanimous decision.

The routine administrative work of the League was carried out by the Permanent Secretariat which was staffed by a relatively small international civil service. In 1921 a fourth organ was added to the League when the Permanent Court of International Justice was set up at the Hague (in the Netherlands) with the task of both advising the Council on legal matters and of judging cases submitted to it by individual states. The League was also committed to setting up a permanent commission to advise the Council on 'all matters relating to the observance of the mandates' and to undertake a whole series of social and economic obligations ranging from maintaining 'fair and humane conditions of labour for men and children' to the international 'prevention and control of disease' (articles 22 & 23).

The heart of the Covenant, articles 8-17, was primarily concerned with the over-riding question of the prevention of war. The League's long-term strategy for creating a peaceful world was summed up in the first section of Article 8:

> The Members of the League recognise that the maintenance of peace requires the reduction of national armaments to the lowest point consistent with national safety, and the enforcement by common action of international obligations.

The process for solving disputes between sovereign powers was defined in articles 12-17. Initially (Article 12) disputes were to be submitted to some form of arbitration or enquiry by the League. While this was happening there was to be a cooling off period of three months. By Article 13 members were committed to carrying out the judgements of the Permanent Court of International Justice or the recommendations of the Council. Even if a dispute was not submitted to arbitration, the Council was empowered by Article 15 to set up an enquiry into its origins. The assumption in these Articles was that states would be only too willing to eliminate war by making use of the League's arbitration machinery. If, however, a state ignored the League's recommendations, Article 16 made it clear that

> 1 1. ... it shall ... be deemed to have committed an act of war against all other Members of the League, which hereby undertake immediately to subject it to the severance of all trade or financial relations ...

5 2. It shall be the duty of the Council in such case to recommend to the several Governments concerned what effective military, naval or air force the Members of the League shall severally contribute to the armed forces to be used to protect the Covenants of the League.

In Article 17 the League's powers were significantly extended by its right to intervene in disputes between non-members of the League, while in Article 11 member states were encouraged to refer to the Assembly or Council any international problem which might threaten the peace.

In theory the League seemed to have formidable powers, but it was not an embryonic 'world state', with powers to coerce independent nations. Its existence was based, as Article 10 made clear, on the recognition of political and territorial independence of all member states. Article 15, for instance, recognised that if a dispute arose from an internal issue, the League had no right to intervene. There were, too, several 'gaps' in the League Covenant, which allowed a potential aggressor to wage war with impunity. War had to be officially declared before the League could act effectively. It had, for instance, no formula for dealing with acts of guerilla warfare, which the instigating state could disown. Even in the event of a formal declaration of war, if the international Court or the Council could not agree on a verdict, then League members, were free, quite 'legally' to continue with their war.

b) The League Struggles to Find a Role

In January 1920 the governments of the Great Powers viewed the League with either cynicism or open hostility. The French doubted its ability to outlaw war, while the Germans saw it as a means for enforcing the hated Versailles Treaty. For a short time after the Republican victory in November 1920 the American government was openly hostile to the League and its officials were instructed to avoid any co-operation with the organisation.

Initially the League had little opportunity to play a major part in either European or world politics. Washington was determined to exclude it from playing any role in solving the post-war problems in the Far East or in finding a solution to the growing Anglo-American naval rivalry (see pages 74-5), while the Allies firmly kept the execution of the Treaty of Versailles in their own hands.

Under the Treaty the League was responsible for the administration of the Saarland and Danzig. This inevitably involved the danger of it becoming too closely associated with the policy of the Allies. Indeed, in the Saarland, it made the mistake of appointing a French chairman to the governing commission which then administered the territory in the interests of France. In Danzig the role of the League was also regarded with great suspicion by the Germans. By Article 101 of the Treaty the

League was to appoint a high commissioner who was to act as a mediator between the Poles and the Danzigers. Inevitably he came to be seen as the agent of the Allies enforcing the Treaty of Versailles. The League was also the guarantor of the agreements, signed by the Allies and the successor states created in 1919, which were aimed at ensuring that the various racial minorities left isolated behind the new frontiers enjoyed full civil rights.

Given the hostility or indifference which initially surrounded the League, it is understandable that in April 1920 the Council decided to concentrate on the less controversial areas where progress could be made. Thus committees were set up to monitor the administration of the mandates and implement the economic and social objectives contained in Article 23. In the long term it was with this work that the League was to be most successful.

c) The Mandates

Article 22 of the Covenant marked a potentially revolutionary new concept in international affairs:

> 1 1. To those colonies and territories, which as a consequence of the late war have ceased to be under the sovereignty of the States which have formerly governed them, and which are inhabited by peoples not yet able to stand by themselves under the strenuous
> 5 conditions of the modern world, there should be applied the principle that the well-being and development of such peoples should form a sacred trust of civilisation, and that securities for the performance of this trust should be embodied in this covenant.

When the Allies distributed the former German and Turkish territories amongst themselves, they were divided into three groups according to how developed they were. The most advanced were in the Middle East, while the most backward were the ex-German islands in the Pacific. The League's greatest task was to avoid becoming a facade for colonialism in a new form. Thus it disputed the South African argument that their mandate over S.W. Africa was 'annexation in all but name'. The mandate powers were required to send in annual reports on their territories to the League's Permanent Mandates Commission, which rapidly gained a formidable reputation for its expertise and authority. Whenever there were riots or disturbances in the mandates, the Commission set up a committee of enquiry which asked searching and sometimes embarrassing questions. For instance, in Palestine the British were criticised for being too pro-Arab in 1930, while the South Africans were censured for their handling of the Bondelzwarts uprising in S.W. Africa in 1923.

The League's attitude towards the mandates was by modern

standards paternalistic and condescending, but nevertheless, as Northedge has argued, 'it helped transform the entire climate of colonialism', since the imperialist powers were forced by moral pressure to consider the interests of the native populations and to begin to contemplate the possibility of their eventual independence.

d) The League's Social and Economic Work

Many League officials were convinced that the gradual forging of international technical, medical and social links would do much to drain the poison out of international politics. According to a contemporary expert on the League, Alfred Zimmern, it was believed that

> 1 Little by little ... the morass of 'high politics' would dry up along its edges, as one issue after another was drained off to Geneva. Thus eventually there would be a world wide co-operative system held together by a network of contacts between government depart-
> 5 ments (other than Foreign Offices), professional organisations and individual experts.

The League was excluded from dealing with the key financial issues of reparations and war debts, but nevertheless in 1922 its Financial Committee was entrusted by the Allied leaders with the task of rebuilding first Austria's and then Hungary's economy. Its Economic Committee had the far greater task of attempting to persuade the powers to abolish their tariffs and create a world-wide free trade zone. It organised two world economic conferences, held in 1927 and 1933, which both Soviet Russia and the United States attended. But not surprisingly, given the strongly protectionist economic climate of the times, it failed to make any progress towards free trade. Its social policy was more successful. One of the greatest successes of the League was the International Labour Organisation (ILO). This had originally been created as an independent organisation by the Treaty of Versailles, but it was financed by the League. In some ways it was a league in miniature. It had its own permanent labour office at Geneva, staffed by a thousand officials. Its work was discussed annually by a conference of labour delegates. Right up to 1939 the ILO turned out an impressive stream of reports, recommendations and statistics which provided important information for a wide range of industries all over the world. The League's Health Organisation provided an invaluable forum for drawing up common policies on such matters as the treatment of diseases, the design of hospitals and health education. The League also set up committees to advise on the limiting of production of opium and other addictive drugs, on the outlawing of the sale of women and children for prostitution and on the effective abolition of slavery.

While the League failed totally in the 1930s in its main objective of keeping the peace, it is often argued that its social, economic and technical work was a real success. It certainly achieved much, but it was long-term work that even today the United Nations has not completed. For instance, its advisory committee on dangerous drugs eventually persuaded member states in 1925 to sign a convention controlling the import and export of drugs. By 1936 54 nations had signed it, but then the outbreak of the Sino-Japanese war in 1937 made it virtually impossible to control the production of drugs in the Far East, which was the major source of them. The success of the work of the ILO is harder to judge. Essentially it existed to inform governments of labour conditions all over the world and to bring to their attention examples of good labour relations. By definition its aim of improving labour relations was very long term indeed. The League's social and economic work was therefore incorporated in the new United Nations and the ILO is still in existence.

e) The League as Peacemaker and Arbitrator, 1920-5

Until 1926 when the foreign ministers of Britain, France and Germany began to attend the meetings of the Council and turn it into a modern Concert of Powers which regularly discussed the main problems of the day, the League of Nation's role in the many post war crises was subordinated to the Supreme Council (of Allied leaders) and the Conference of Ambassadors, which had been set up to supervise the carrying out of the Treaty of Versailles. For the most part it therefore dealt with minor crises only.

In 1920 the inability of the League to act effectively without the backing of the Great Powers was clearly demonstrated. In May Persia appealed to the League for assistance when Soviet forces occupied the Persian port of Enzeli. Fortunately for the League, as it was unsupported in this issue by any Great Power, the appeal could be dismissed on the grounds that negotiations were already in fact taking place between Moscow and Teheran. The League also failed to protect Armenia from a joint Russo-Turkish attack, even though the Supreme Council had played with the idea of making it a mandate, as again none of the Great Powers were ready to protect it with force. One of the French delegates caustically observed in the Assembly that he and his colleagues were

> in the ridiculous position of an Assembly which considers what steps should be taken, though it is perfectly aware that it is impossible for them to be carried out.

In October 1920 in response to appeals from the Polish Foreign Minister the League negotiated an armistice between Poland and Lithuania, whose quarrel over border territories was rapidly escalating into war. The ceasefire did not, however, hold, as shortly afterwards

General Zeligowski with a Polish force, which the Warsaw government diplomatically pretended was acting on its own initiative, occupied the city of Vilna and set up the new puppet Government of Central Lithuania under his protection. The League first called for a plebiscite and then, when this was rejected, attempted in vain to negotiate a compromise settlement. In March 1922 Poland finally annexed Vilna province. A year later, after it was obvious that the League could not impose a solution without the support of the Great Powers, the Conference of Ambassadors took the matter into its own hands and recognised Polish sovereignty over Vilna. Britain, France and Italy, by failing to use the machinery of the League to stop Polish aggression, had again effectively marginalised it.

In less intractable disputes, where the states involved were willing to accept a verdict, the League did have an important role to play as mediator. The League enjoyed a rare success in the dispute between Finland and Sweden over the Aaland Islands. These had belonged to the Grand Duchy of Finland when she had been part of the Russian Empire. Once she had broken away from Russia in 1917, the islanders, who were ethnically Swedish, appealed to Stockholm to take over the islands. When Sweden began to threaten force, the British referred the matter to the League. In 1921 the League supported the status quo by leaving the islands under Finnish sovereignty, but insisted on itself ensuring the civil rights of the Swedish population there. Neither government liked the verdict, but both accepted it and, what is more important, made it work.

In the second half of 1921 the League did serve as a useful means of focusing the attention of the Great Powers on the plight of Albania when she urgently appealed for help against Greek and Yugoslav aggression. As the Conference of Ambassadors had not yet finally fixed her frontiers, the Greeks and Yugoslavs were exploiting the ambiguous situation to occupy as much Albanian territory as they could. The Council responded by despatching a commission of enquiry, but it took a telegram from Lloyd George both to galvanise the Conference of Ambassadors into finalising the frontiers and to push the League Council into threatening economic sanctions against Yugoslavia if she did not recognise them. When this was successful, the League was then entrusted with supervising the Yugoslav withdrawal. Thus in this crisis the League had played a useful but again secondary role to the Allied powers. The fact that the Conference of Ambassadors then made Italy the protector of Albania's independence indicates where the real power lay.

In August 1921 the League played a key role in masking a British retreat over the Upper Silesian plebiscite. A bitter Anglo-French dispute over its interpretation was referred to the League Council (pages 46-7), which decided in favour of the French. The League again proved useful in the protracted dispute over Memel. When the Lithuanians objected to the decision by the Conference of Ambassadors to internationalise the port of Memel, which the Treaty of Versailles had originally intended to cede to Lithuania, and seized the port themselves in 1923, the League was the obvious body to sort out the problem. Its decision for Lithuania was accepted by the Allies.

Attempts by Britain and Sweden to refer the major crisis of 1923, the Ruhr occupation, to the League were blocked by the French, who had no intention of allowing the League to mediate between themselves and the Germans. In the Corfu incident of August-September 1923 the League's efforts to intervene were yet again blocked by a Great Power. The crisis was triggered by the assassination of three Italians in Greek territory near the Albanian frontier, who were part of an Allied team tracing the Albanian frontiers for the Conference of Ambassadors. Mussolini, the Italian Fascist Prime Minister, who had come to power the preceding October, immediately seized the chance to issue a deliberately unacceptable ultimatum to Athens. When the Greeks rejected three of its demands, Italian troops occupied Corfu. The Greeks wanted to refer the incident to the League, while Salandra, the Italian Foreign Minister, was adamant that the Conference of Ambassadors should deal with it. The Conference while initially accepting some assistance from the League, nevertheless ultimately settled the case itself and insisted that Greece should pay 50 million lire compensation to Italy. Once this was agreed, Italian forces were withdrawn from Corfu. The Corfu incident, like the Ruhr crisis, underlined the continuing ability of the Great Powers to ignore the League and to take unilateral action when it pleased them.

In 1924 the League was confronted with another crisis involving a greater Power and a lesser Power. On this occasion it was able to mediate successfully. It provided a face-saving means of retreat for Turkey in her dispute with Britain over the future of Mosul, which according to the Treaty of Lausanne (see page 43) was to be decided by direct Anglo-Turkish negotiations. When these talks broke down and the British issued in October 1924 an ultimatum to Turkey to withdraw her forces within 48 hours, the League intervened and successfully recommended a line of temporary demarcation behind which the Turkish forces withdrew. There followed a commission of enquiry to consult the local Kurdish population, which, as total independence was not an option, preferred British to Turkish rule. The League's recommendation that Mosul should become a mandate of Iraq for 25 years was then accepted. As Iraq was a British mandate, this effectively put it under British control.

In October 1925, at a time when the League Council was beginning to turn into a Concert of Powers, the League's handling of the Greeco-Bulgarian conflict, like its solution to the Aaland Island dispute, was to be a rare example of a complete success. When the Bulgarians appealed to the Council, its request for a ceasefire was heeded immediately by both sides. So too was the verdict of its commission of enquiry, which found in favour of Bulgaria. It was an impressive example of what the League could do, and in the autumn of 1925 this success, together with the new 'Locarno spirit', seemed to auger well for the future. Briand stressed at the meeting of the Council in October 1925:

> 1 It had been shown that the criticisms which had been brought against the League of Nations to the effect that its machinery was cumbersome and that it found it difficult to take action in circumstances which required an urgent solution were unjustified.
> 5 It has been proved that a nation which appealed to the League when it felt that its existence was threatened, could be sure that the Council would be at its post ready to undertake its work of conciliation.

The League was not put to the test again until the Manchurian crisis of 1931. Unfortunately Briand's optimism was to be shown to be premature.

6 The League, America and Disarmament

One of the major tasks of the League was to work out an acceptable world disarmament programme. At first the Council delegated this work to the Temporary Mixed Commission. One of its proposals envisaged devising ratios between the land forces of the League's members, but this was rapidly rejected when it emerged that the smaller states would have no army at all! It soon became clear that disarmament could not be divorced from the question of security, for if a state did not feel secure, it would hardly disarm. Thus on the initiative of the French the Assembly adopted a resolution in September 1922 which specifically linked these two aims. In 1924 the League did attempt to draft an ambitious collective security agreement, the Geneva Protocol (see pages 57-8), but it was rejected by Britain, who feared that it would commit her to policing the world. Britain preferred more precise regional agreements, or as Austen Chamberlain put it: 'special arrangements to meet special needs'.

Chamberlain was primarily thinking of Locarno when he made this remark, but with America outside the League the twin problems of growing Anglo-American naval rivalry and deteriorating American-Japanese relations in the Pacific had also been tackled on a largely regional basis. In 1919 America had been alarmed by the rise of Japanese power in the Pacific. Japan, who already possessed the third largest navy in the world, had begun a major naval construction programme. The Americans responded by forming a Pacific fleet and embarking on their own formidable building programme, which, when completed, would make the American navy the largest in the world. In turn this pushed Britain in early 1921 into announcing her own naval programme, but privately she intimated to Washington that she desired a negotiated settlement as she could not afford a naval race. President Harding was anxious both to reduce armaments and to economise, but he would only negotiate with Britain if she agreed not to prolong the 20-year-old Anglo-Japanese alliance, which theoretically at least, could have involved Britain as Japan's ally in a war against America. As the treaty was due for renewal in July 1921 the British and Japanese agreed under pressure from Washington to replace it by a new four Power treaty, which committed Britain, France, Japan and the USA to respect each others possessions in the Pacific and to refer any dispute arising out of this agreement to a conference of the four signatory Powers.

With the Anglo-Japanese Treaty out of the way, the first Washington Treaty was signed in February 1922 for a duration of 14 years. It halted the building of capital ships for ten years, provided for the scrapping of certain battle ships and battlecruisers, and, for those capital ships which were spared the breaker's yard, established a ratio of 3 for Japan and 1.67 each for Italy and France to every five for Britain and the United States. In 1929 Britain, Japan and the United States in the London Naval Treaty agreed to extend the main principle of this agreement to smaller fighting ships.

From 1922 onwards the United States' attitude towards the League began to alter. She saw the value of participating in some of the League's committees on social, economic and health matters, and President Harding even considered American membership of the Permanent Court of International Justice in 1923, but in a bitter battle lasting up to 1935 the Senate defeated it. When the League set up a Preparatory Commission in 1926 to prepare for a world disarmament conference both the United States and Soviet Russia participated, but the American Government also pursued its own distinctive approach towards disarmament. Peace movements, especially the 'American Committee for the Outlawry of War' and the Carnegie Endowment for International Peace, exerted considerable pressure on the American Government. In March 1927, Professor Shotwell, a director of the Carnegie Endowment, on a visit to Paris persuaded Briand to sign a message and send it over the head of the President to the American people, proposing a Franco-American pact that would outlaw war. Briand was, of course, delighted at any chance to involve America, even if indirectly, in the French post-war alliance system. To avoid just such a linkage Kellogg, the American secretary of State, replied cautiously in December suggesting a general pact between as many states as possible, rejecting war 'as an instrument of national policy'. Briand had no alternative but to accept it, if he wished to ensure American co-operation. Thus on 27 August 1928 the Kellogg-Briand Peace Pact was signed by 15 states, and by 1933 a further 50 had 'adhered' to it. It consisted of three articles only:

1 1. The high contracting parties solemnly declare in the names of their respective peoples that they condemn recourse to war for the solution of international controversies, and renounce it as an instrument of national policy in their relations with one another.
5 2. The high contracting parties agree that the settlement or solution of all disputes or conflicts of whatever nature or of whatever origin they may be, which may arise among them, shall never be sought except by pacific means.
3. This treaty ...shall remain open ... for adherence by all the other
10 Powers of the world.

Optimists saw the Pact as supplementing the Covenant. It outlawed war, while the League had the necessary machinery for setting up commissions of inquiry and implementing cooling off periods in the event of a dispute. Pessimists, however, pointed to the fact that it was just a general declaration of intention with no binding clauses. Perhaps in reality all that could be said for it was that it would give the American Government a moral basis on which it could intervene in world affairs, should it desire to do so. In 1946 the pact provided the legal basis for charging the Nazi leaders with the crime of waging aggressive war at the Nuremberg trials.

In 1930 the Preparatory Commission, at last after protracted discussions on different models of disarmament, produced its final draft for an international convention. The League Council called the long awaited World Disarmament Conference in February 1932 at Geneva. It could not have been convened at a more unfortunate time: the Manchurian crisis was ecalating into full-scale war between China and Japan (see pages 83-5), the rise of nationalism in Germany was making France and Poland less likely to compromise over German demands for equality in armaments, while the impact of the Depression on the United States was reviving the isolationist tendencies of the early 1920s. Long before the Germans withdrew in November 1933 (page 88) it was clear that the Conference would fail.

7 Was the Failure of the Politics of Reconciliation Inevitable?

In the immediate aftermath of the Second World War it was tempting to trace links between the foreign policy of Stresemann, Brüning and Hitler and conclude that the Locarno era was doomed to failure. Locarno did create for a time a new atmosphere, but it could not for ever obscure the realities of European diplomacy. Germany under any government was determined to revise the Treaty of Versailles and regain, albeit peacefully, with Stresemann and Brüning, as much of her former power as she could, while France inevitably feared this and constantly sought security against the ever present German threat. The absence of an unambiguous Anglo-American guarantee of French security continued therefore to be one of the main causes of European instability.

A.J.P. Taylor cynically observed that: 'Rival states can be frightened into friendship only by the shadow of some greater danger'. Does this mean then that without immense Soviet pressure on western Europe, as occurred after 1945, Franco-German rivalry would have led Europe into another war, even if Hitler had never become German Chancellor? In 1930 few Europeans would have agreed that war was inevitable. The German Nationalists, for instance, had been routed in the Young Referendum, and anti-war feeling was widespread in Britain, France and Germany. Perhaps Briand's plan for a common market in which the European economies would have become inter-dependent pointed to one way of escape from national rivalries. Certainly an important condition for European peace was continuing prosperity, which arguably in time would have eroded both German resentments and French fears. The Depression, however, by devastating the German economy and producing an electoral backlash that brought Hitler to power, pushed Germany into pursuing policies against which armed alliances rather than the Locarno spirit would be effective.

Making notes on the 'The Politics of Reconciliation, 1924-30'

Essentially this chapter is concerned with the improvement in international relations that took place between 1924 and 1930. While reading this chapter you should ask yourself whether the Dawes Plan, the Locarno Agreements and the Kellogg Pact laid the foundations for a workable post-war international system or whether the whole Versailles system together with the League was doomed to collapse by 1930. The following headings and sub-headings should provide a suitable framework for your notes:

1 Introduction: Stresemann, Briand and Chamberlain
2 The Dawes Plan
3 The French search for security
4 Locarno
4.1 What was the 'Locarno spirit'?
4.2 The Young Plan and the Allied evacuation of the Rhineland
4.3 Briand's European union plan. Could it have worked?
5 Eastern Europe: Soviet Russia, Poland and the Balkans
6 The League of Nations
6.1 Its constitution and how it worked
6.2 Its attempt to find a role
6.3 The mandates
6.4 Its social and economic work
6.5 How effective were its attempts to prevent war?
7 Disarmament
7.1 The League's early efforts

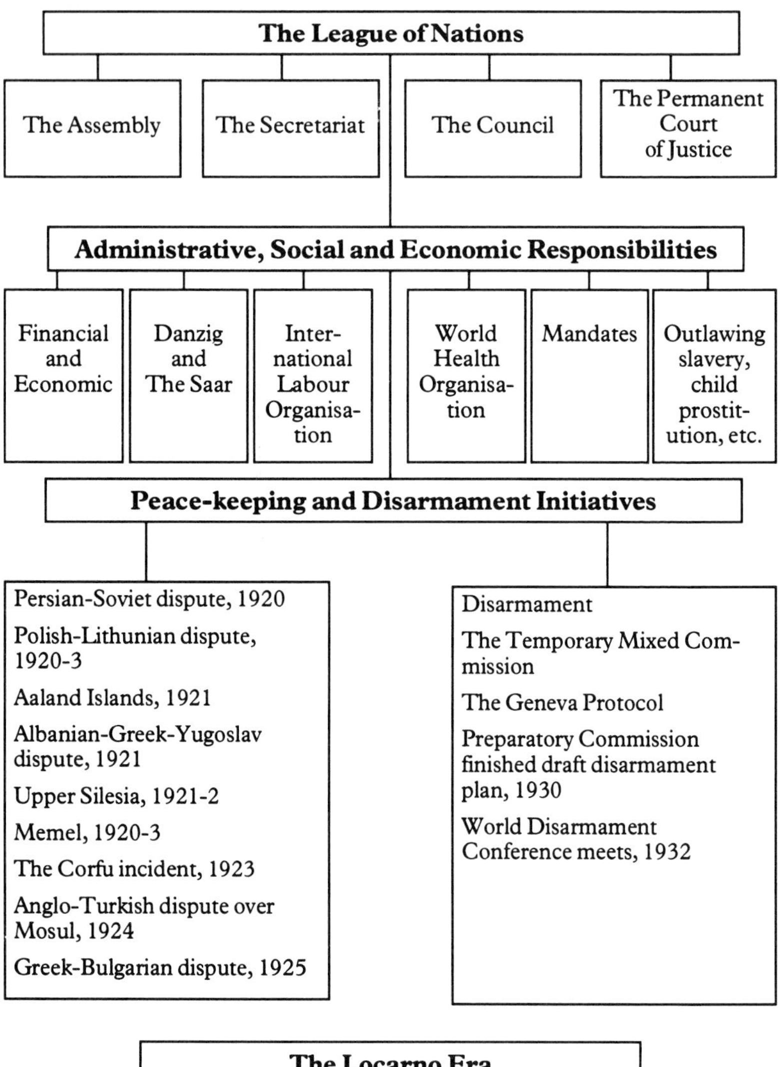

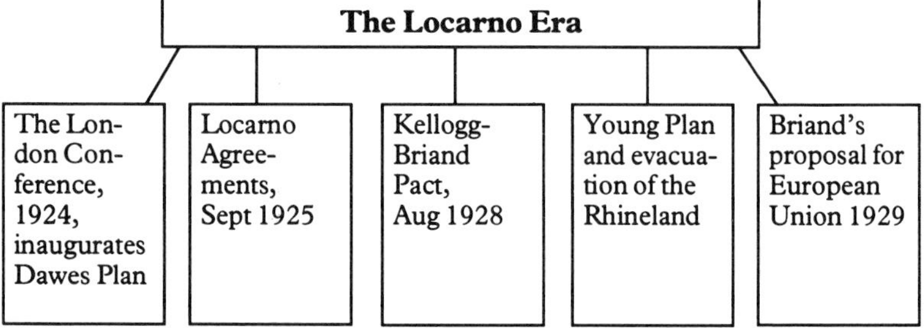

Summary - The Politics of Reconciliation, 1924-30

7.2 The Washington Treaty
7.3 The Kellogg-Briand Pact
7.4 The World Disarmament Conference
8 Conclusion: Could the Locarno era survive?

Answering essay questions on *'The Politics of Reconciliation, 1924-30'*

In preparing essay questions on this topic, it is important to bear three main themes in mind: the extent to which the peace treaties were modified by 1930, the role and effectiveness of the League of Nations, 1919-30 and whether the improvement in relations between Britain, France and Germany was firmly based. Questions on all three topics appear regularly in both the more general outline and specialised papers.
Look at the following questions:

1. How far by 1929 did the impact on Europe of the post-war settlements of 1919-23 disappoint the hopes of the peace-makers?
2. When and why did the peace settlements of 1919-23 begin to break down?
3. To what extent can one argue that the break-up of the Austro-Hungarian Empire after the First World War caused more problems than it solved?
4. Why and with what consequences for Europe in the years up to 1929 did the victors of the First World War support the principle of national independence in Central Europe?
5. Why was there a mood of optimism and co-operation in Europe between 1925 and 1929 and why did it prove only temporary?
6. Why did relations improve between Britain, France and Germany, 1924-9?
7. Why was the League of Nations unable to fulfil the hopes it inspired when it was founded?
8. Why was the League unable to deal effectively with international aggression?
9. What problems confronted the League of Nations in the years 1919-29 and to what extent was it successful in promoting the cause of peace?
10. What did the League of Nations achieve?

In preparing these questions it will quickly become clear that you will need to look back at your notes on chapter 3. Questions 1 and 2 are both fairly straightforward and require you to discuss why the peace settlements failed, but do not forget that the examiner will expect you to be able to handle a lot of complex information in an analytical way. Above all you must be ready to question what such statements as 'disappoint' and 'begin to break down' mean. Questions 3 and 4 require a detailed knowledge of events in central Europe and the Balkans. Before starting such questions be sure that you really do know your facts. In question 3, for example, you will need not only to know the details of the Treaties of St. Germain, Neuilly and Trianon but also to be able to trace the rivalries of the successor states to Austria-Hungary and the attempts of the French to build an alliance system in eastern Europe. Questions on the Locarno era usually require you to account for the improvement in relations between Britain, France and Germany after 1924 (question 6), but you are often also asked why this improvement was short lived (question 5). Was it just the Depression or would Franco-German relations have inevitably deteriorated as Germany recovered her strength? You may want to return to this question again after reading chapter 5.

Questions on the League usually fall into two main categories: they either focus on its failure to stop aggression (questions 7 and 8) or on its achievements (question 10). In dealing with the first type of question you will need, of course, to analyse the relevant parts of its constitution, the impact of America's absence as well as the frequent reluctance of the Powers to take it seriously, but you will also need to read about its failure in the Manchurian and Abyssinian crises (see chapter 5.) It is unusual for examiners to limit a question on the difficulties facing the League to the period 1919-29, although it sometimes happens (question 9)! If the question is more concerned with the achievements of the League (question 10), then its first ten years will provide the bulk of the material for your answer. In preparation for answering this question you might like to draw up a list of the League's achievements in its social and economic work as well as in its prevention of conflict in the 1920s.

Source-based questions on *'The Politics of Reconciliation, 1924-30'*

1 From Dawes to Locarno, 1924-5

Read carefully the extracts from the statement by the Treasury on page 56, Chamberlain's speech on page 58 and Stresemann's letter to the Crown Prince on page 61 and then answer the following questions:

a) How does the extract on page 56 help us to understand why the British government welcomed the Dawes Plan? (3 marks)
b) What does Chamberlain mean when he says 'for which no British government will or ever can risk the bones of a British grenadier' (lines3-4)? (2 marks)
c) Read the extracts from Chamberlain's speech and Stresemann's letter. What light do they shed on British and German foreign policy and what are their implications for French security? (10 marks)

2 The 'Locarno Spirit', 1925-30

Read carefully Briand's speech to the League of Nations on page 63 and the clauses of the Kellogg-Briand Pact on page 76 and then study the cartoon on page 60. Answer the following questions:

a) What light does Briand's speech to the League of Nations shed on the aims of French foreign policy? (5 marks)
b) Explain the meaning of Point 2 of the Kellogg-Briand Pact (lines 5-8). (2 marks)
c) What is the significance of the empty cupboard in the cartoon? (3 marks)
d) Using these documents and any other evidence known to you consider whether the cartoonist's prediction was confirmed by international developments between 1925-30. (10 marks)

3 The work of the League of Nations (1)

Carefully read the extracts from the British commentary (page 66), the extract from Article 16 (page 67-8), the remark by a French delegate to the League Assembly (page 71), and the extract from Briand's speech of October 1925 (page 74). Answer the following questions:

a) What does the British official commentary mean by 'trust in the influence of custom to mould opinion' (lines 4-5)? (3 marks)
b) From a comparison of the British commentary and the statement by the French delegate assess the potential effectiveness of Article 16. (7 marks)
c) Using these documents and any other evidence known to you consider the view that the League after initial 'teething troubles' was a success in the 1920s. (10 Marks)

4 The work of the League of Nations (2)

Carefully read Article 22 of the League constitution on page 69 and Professor Zimmern's commentary on page 70. Answer the following questions:

a) Explain what is meant in Article 22 by 'peoples not yet able to stand by themselves under the strenuous conditions of the modern world' (lines 4-5). (2 marks)
b) Explain how the League attempted to safeguard the well being and development of such peoples. (6 marks)
c) What does Zimmern mean by '... the morass of "high politics" would dry up along its edges' (lines 1-2)? (2 marks)
d Do these documents support the view that the League was a considerable success in its social and economic work? (10 marks)

CHAPTER 5

The Impact of the Great Depression on International Politics

1 Introduction

The Great Depression, triggered by the Wall Street Crash, marked a turning point in inter-war history. Not only did it weaken the economic and social stability of the world's major Powers, but it also dealt a devastating blow to the progress made since 1924 towards creating a new framework for peaceful international co-operation. It has been called by Robert Boyce 'the third global catastrophe of the century'. It is hard to exaggerate its international impact. Between 1929 and 1932 the volume of world trade fell by 70 per cent. Unemployment rose to 13 million in the United States, to 6 million in Germany and to 3 million in Britain. Japan was particularly hard hit: some 50 per cent of her mining and heavy industrial capacity was forced to close and the collapse of the American market virtually destroyed her large and lucrative export trade in silk.

Inevitably an economic crisis on this scale had a decisive political impact. In Germany it brought Hitler to power and in Japan it strengthened the hand of an influential group of army officers who argued that only by seizing Manchuria could Japan ride out the slump. In Italy it prompted Mussolini to have plans drawn up for the conquest of Abyssinia. The Depression's impact on the politics of the three democracies was equally disastrous. It delayed both their rearmament programmes and created an international climate in which each of the three Powers suspected that the other was the cause of its financial and economic difficulties. Consequently, during the years of 1929-34, the Depression prevented any effective collaboration between them at a time when it was vital to deter the aggressive nationalism of Japan and Germany.

As international trade collapsed the Great Powers erected tariff barriers and attempted to make themselves economically self-sufficient. The British and the French with their huge empires had a decisive advantage over the Germans, Italians and Japanese, who increasingly began to assert their right to carve out their own empires, spheres of interest or 'Lebensraum' (living space) as Hitler called it. The Depression encouraged a dangerously competitive nationalism which was neatly summed up in 1936 by Hitler in The Four Year Plan Memorandum:

> Politics are the conduct and the course of the historical struggle for life. The aim of these struggles is survival.

2 The Manchurian Crisis

Arguably, the Japanese occupation of Manchuria in 1931 was a continuation of policies followed by Japanese governments since the defeat of Russia in 1905 when Japan had been awarded the lease of the South Manchurian Railway and the right to protect it with some 15,000 troops. In the late 1920s these concessions were threatened by the course of the Chinese civil war. In 1928 Chiang Kai-shek, the leader of the Chinese Nationalists, had occupied Peking. The Japanese army feared that the local Chinese War Lord, who controlled most of

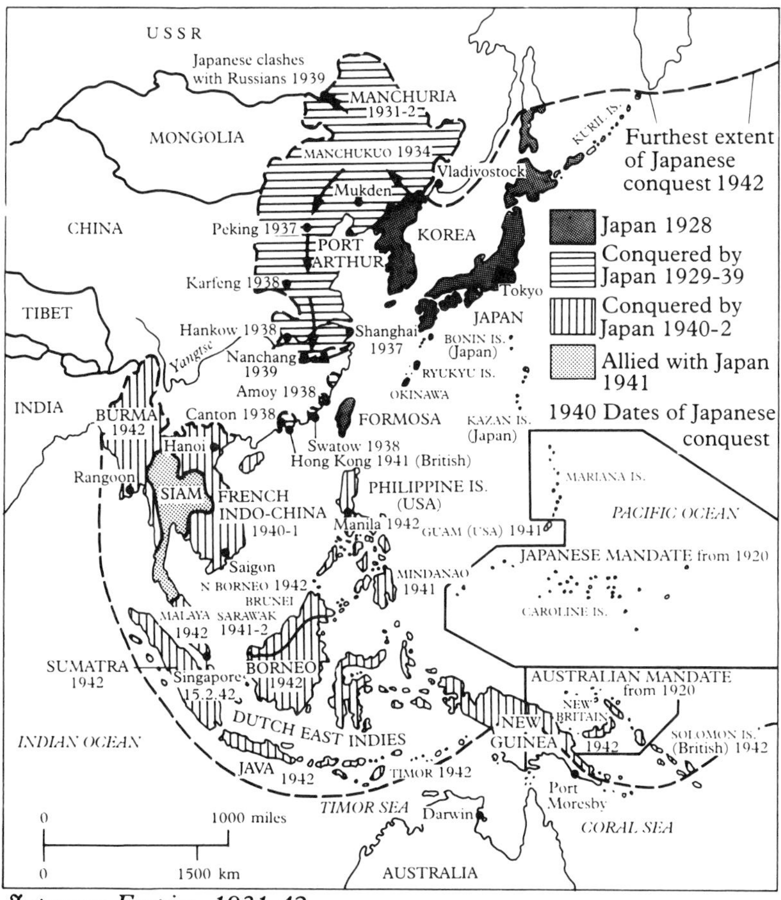

Japanese Empire, 1931-42

Manchuria, would rally to Chiang Kai-shek and began to draw up plans to strengthen their hold on the province. Initially the Tokyo government was strong enough to restrain the army. However, its impotence in the face of the onset of the Depression strengthened its critics, amongst whom both the officer corps and the patriotic societies played a major role. In November 1930 the Japanese Prime Minister was shot by a member of one of the patriotic societies and in the following March plans, which were only cancelled at the last moment, were drawn up for a military coup.

Collectively these events combined to convince the army in Manchuria that it would have to act decisively if Japan was to preserve both her influence and access to the important sources of coal and metallic ores there at a time when economic protectionism was already making it difficult for her to purchase vital raw materials elsewhere. Consequently it decided to devise an incident which would provide the pretext for it to act. On 18 September 1931 a bomb exploded on the railway line just outside Mukden where both local Chinese and Japanese troops were stationed. This was immediately blamed on the Chinese and provided the Japanese forces with the desired excuse to occupy not only Mukden but the whole of southern Manchuria. China immediately appealed to the League of Nations, but the Council's response was cautious and dilatory. It first asked Japan to withdraw her troops back into the railway zone and then, when this was ignored, sent a commission of enquiry under the chairmanship of Lord Lytton. The Japanese completed the occupation of Manchuria and turned it into the satellite state of Manchukuo while the Lytton Commission was conducting a leisurely fact finding operation in the spring of 1932.

It is easy to criticise the League for not acting more decisively, but without the commitment of the Great Powers it was not in the position to take effective action. Neither of the two most important naval powers, Britain and the USA, were ready to use force against Japan. From the Japanese point of view the timing of the Mukden incident could not have been better. Britain was pushed off the Gold Standard on 20 September and shortly afterwards a minor mutiny at the naval base at Invergordon, caused by a cut in the sailors' wages, threatened temporarily to paralyse the Royal Navy. America, shell-shocked by the Depression, was unwilling to do more than denounce Japanese aggression. She did, however, send a representative to the League Council in October 1931, but it rapidly emerged that he was there only as an observer. It is sometimes argued that the British government and powerful City interests secretly supported Japan. It is true that Britain did have some sympathy with Japanese action in Manchuria. Like Japan she had vital commercial interests in China which she felt were threatened by the rise of Chinese nationalism. Britain also appreciated Japan's potential role in providing a barrier against the spread of Bolshevism from Russia into northern China. Nevertheless, the real reason why Britain was not ready to urge more decisive action against Japan was that neither her government nor her people desired to fight a war on an issue that was not central to British interests. In February 1933 Sir John Simon, the Foreign Minister, told the House of Commons:

1 I think I am myself enough of a pacifist to take the view that however we handle the matter, I do not intend my own country to get into trouble about it ... There is one great difference between 1914 and now and it is this: in no circumstances will this
5 Government authorise this country to be party to this struggle.

It was not until September that the League received the Commission's report. Although it conceded that the treaty rights which Japan had enjoyed in Manchuria since 1905 had made Sino-Japanese friction unavoidable, it nevertheless emphasised that

1 without a declaration of war a large area of what was indisputably Chinese territory has been forcibly seized and occupied by the armed forces of Japan and has in consequence of this operation been separated from and declared independent of the rest of
5 China.

The Commission stressed that the problem of Manchuria could only be solved by a general improvement in Sino-Japanese relations and proposed that, after Japanese troops had been withdrawn back into the railway zone, both China and Japan should negotiate not only a treaty guaranteeing Japan's rights in Manchuria but also non-aggression and trade agreements.

Essentially then the report was erroneously based on the assumption that the Japanese had no territorial designs in China and were ready to compromise over Manchuria. When it was adopted unanimously, with the single exception of Japan, by the League Assembly on 24 February 1933, Japan withdrew from the League. It was obvious that only armed intervention by the Great Powers would now be able to force her out of Manchuria, and that option was not politically realistic in 1933.

The Japanese occupation of Manchuria changed the balance of power in the Pacific. Japan had broken free from the restraints imposed upon her at the Washington Conference in 1922 by Britain and America (see page 75) and had preserved her access to valuable coal and iron ore resources. Above all she was in a favourable strategic position to widen the war against China. The Manchurian incident is often seen as the first link in a chain of events that led to the Second World War. However, although it did weaken the League and the whole idea of collective security, it did not necessarily signal the end of the Versailles system in Europe. The Abyssinian crisis (see pages 96-7) was to play a far more important part in its destruction.

3 German Foreign Policy, 1930-5

Was 1930 or 1933 the more significant turning point in German foreign policy? In March 1930 Heinrich Brüning was appointed Chancellor of a minority government supported by the German Nationalists. Only months after the acceptance of the Young Plan (see page 110) he was determined not only to end reparation payments but also to assert Germany's right to rearm and to free herself from the remaining restrictions of the Treaty of Versailles. To achieve these aims Brüning pursued a hazardous strategy. He attempted an independent solution to Germany's economic problems by savage cuts in government expenditure rather than accept in 1931 a French loan to which political conditions were attached. This maximised the impact of the Depression and pushed up unemployment levels. Inevitably Germany's economic misery increased support for the Nazi Party which in the elections of September 1930 became a major political force in the *Reichstag*. At the same time Brüning secretly encouraged the Nazi Party's strident opposition to Versailles so that he could put added pressure on Britain and France to make concessions. Brüning and his two successors, Papen and Schleicher, created what Professor Hiden has called 'the diplomatic-military instruments which Hitler was able to use in the early stages of his regime'. Hitler was able to reassure the European Powers and his own diplomats, at least until 1935, that he was only following the revisionist policies of his immediate predecessors.

a) The Foreign Policy of Brüning, Papen and Schleicher

The change in German foreign policy was evident in the summer of 1930 when Brüning seized upon proposals first put forward by the Austrian government for a customs union with Germany. In a cabinet discussion in July Brüning argued that Germany needed 'an adequate natural area of living space'. The plan was opposed bitterly by the French who feared that a customs union would inevitably lead to a political union, which was contrary to both the Treaties of St Germain and Versailles (see chapter 3). Thus, when Germany was plunged into a major banking crisis caused by the collapse of the Viennese *Credit-Anstalt,* the French blocked every proposal for an emergency loan until Germany not only renounced the customs union, but also abandoned attempts to revise reparations for at least five years. Ultimately the sheer weakness of the German and Austrian economies forced Brüning to refer the whole plan to the League's Permanent Court of Arbitration at the Hague. This ruled in September 1931 that the proposed customs union was contrary to Austria's treaty obligations. Ironically the banking crisis helped Brüning ultimately achieve his over-riding aim of abolishing reparations. In July 1931 a proposal put forward by President Hoover for a year's moratorium on all international debts was accepted by the Great Powers. Brüning used this year to convince the Americans and British that the payment of reparations was no longer a realistic option by stressing both Germany's financial weakness and the strength of Nationalist opposition to it. Brüning was largely successful although he was forced to resign a month before the Powers agreed at the Lausanne Conference in June 1932 effectively to cancel reparations altogether.

At the World Disarmament Conference which first met in February 1932 the time was again right for a determined German initiative. The western democracies were divided and uncertain. The French had an ambitious programme for allocating national forces to a League police force for peace-keeping operations, while America and Britain viewed this potentially open-ended commitment with alarm. Brüning insisted on Germany achieving equality of armaments with the other major European powers either by them disarming down to the German level or by allowing Germany to rearm up to their's. That Brüning was really thinking of the latter solution was shown by his proposals for doubling the German army. After months of heated debate and a German threat to walk out of the conference, a face saving formula was devised whereby Germany's 'equality of rights' would be recognised within 'a system which would provide security for all nations'. Significantly, in November, the German War Ministry finalised a plan for large increases in the army by 1938.

b) Hitler

The tempo of the German campaign against Versailles quickened once Hitler came to power in 1933, although for two years at least he appeared to pursue the same policy as Brüning, albeit somewhat more vigorously and unconventionally. Was he then just following the traditional policy of making Germany 'the greatest power in Europe from her natural weight' by exploiting every opportunity that presented itself, as A.J.P. Taylor argued?

In his book, *Mein Kampf*, written in 1924, Hitler was quite specific about the main thrust of Nazi foreign policy:

> 1 And so we National Socialists consciously draw a line beneath the foreign policy tendency of our pre-war period. We take up where we broke off six hundred years ago. We stop the endless German movement to the south and west and turn our gaze towards the
> 5 land in the east. At long last we break off the colonial and commercial policy of the pre-war period and shift to the soil policy of the future. If we speak of soil in Europe, we can primarily have in mind only Russia and her vassal border states.

Was this still an aim in 1933 or was it just a pipe dream long since forgotten? There are distinguished historians such as Hans Mommsen who doubt whether Hitler had a consistent foreign policy of 'unchanging ... priorities' and argue that it was usually determined by economic pressures and demands for action from within the Nazi Party itself. Other historians, particularly those of the 'Programme School', take a diametrically opposed line and argue on the strength of *Mein Kampf* and Hitler's Secret Book (published in 1928) that he planned first to defeat France and Russia, and then after building up a large navy make a determined bid for world power even if it involved war against both Britain and the United States. The history of Nazi foreign policy generates such controversy because Hitler's actions were so often ambiguous and contradictory. Despite this there is currently a general consensus among historians that Hitler did intend to wage a series of wars which would ultimately culminate in a struggle for global hegemony. Alan Bullock has argued that the key to understanding Hitler's foreign policy is that he combined 'consistency of aim with complete opportunism in method and tactics'.

In 1933 Hitler's immediate priorities were to consolidate the Nazi take-over of power and to re-build Germany's military strength. This would eventually put him in a position to destroy what remained of the Versailles system. However, whilst rearming he had to be careful not to provoke an international backlash. He therefore followed a cautious policy of avoiding risks and defusing potential opposition, while gradually withdrawing Germany from any multilateral commitments which might prevent him from pursuing an independent policy. He hoped particularly to isolate France by negotiating alliances with Britain and Italy. He was naturally anxious to extricate Germany from the World Disarmament Conference, but was careful to wait until the autumn before he risked both withdrawing from the Conference and the League of Nations. He had first skilfully reassured Britain and Italy of his peaceful intentions by signing the Four Power Pact, proposed by Mussolini, which aimed at revising Versailles through joint agreement of the Great Powers. Although on the face of it this seemed to limit Germany's freedom of action, Hitler calculated, correctly as it turned out, that the French would never ratify it.

Hitler's first major initiative in foreign policy was the conclusion of the German-Polish Non-aggression Pact. He did this despite opposition from the German Foreign Office which wanted to maintain good relations with Soviet Russia. This seriously weakened France's security system in eastern Europe, as she had relied upon her alliance with Poland to contain Germany. Nevertheless, Germany still remained very vulnerable. Hitler was warned in August 1934 by a senior German diplomat, B. W. von Bülow that

1 In judging the situation we should never overlook the fact that no kind of rearmament in the next few years could give us military

> security. Even apart from our isolation, we shall for a long time yet be hopelessly inferior to France in the military sphere. A
> 5 particularly dangerous period will be 1934-5 on account of the re-organisation of the *Reichswehr* [Army].

Hitler was certainly aware of this danger but over Austria he adopted a more provocative line, possibly because he assumed that Austria was really a domestic German affair. In June 1934 he tried to convince Mussolini, at a meeting with him in Venice, that Austria should become in effect a German satellite. When Mussolini rejected this, Hitler risked in July giving the Austrian Nazis strong unofficial encouragement to stage what turned out to be a disastrously unsuccessful uprising in Vienna. Mussolini, who was determined to keep Austria as a buffer state between Italy and Germany immediately mobilised troops on the Brenner frontier and forced Hitler to disown the coup. The incident brought about a sharp deterioration in German-Italian relations and appeared to rule out any prospect of an alliance. In March 1935 Hitler took another risk when he announced the re-introduction of conscription despite the fears of his advisers that this would lead to French intervention. Superficially these fears appeared to be confirmed when in April the British, French and Italian heads of government met at Stresa and both condemned German rearmament and resolved to maintain the peace settlements. Hitler, however, quickly launched a diplomatic offensive to reassure the Powers of his peaceful intentions. In a speech that in places appeared to echo the language of the League of Nations he proposed a series of non-aggression pacts with Germany's neighbours, promised to observe Locarno and accept an over-all limitation on armaments. He also offered Britain an agreement limiting the German fleet to 35 per cent of the total strength of the Royal Navy. He concluded with an apparently deep commitment to peace and reconstruction:

> 1 Whoever lights the torch of war in Europe can wish for nothing but chaos. We, however, can live in the firm conviction that in our time will be fulfilled, not the decline, but the renaissance of the West. That Germany may make an imperishable contribution to this
> 5 great work is our proud hope and unshakable belief.

His tactics were partly successful. Britain did rise to the bait and accept Hitler's terms for an Anglo-German naval convention in June 1935. This appeared to give British approval to German re-armament and broke up the unity of the Stresa Front. On the other hand there were signs in the summer of 1935 that France's efforts to contain Germany were beginning to be successful. She was able to exploit Mussolini's opposition to Hitler's ambitions in Austria to negotiate a Franco-Italian agreement in January 1935. By June the two Powers were holding joint military staff talks, while on 2 May the Franco-Russian Pact was signed (see page 92).

4 The Reaction of the Great Powers to Nazi Germany, 1933-5

For the Great Powers 1933-5 was a period in which they had to come to terms with the reality of Nazi Germany. In 1933, even though Germany was only just beginning to rearm, her strength was potentially far greater than in 1914 as it was enhanced by a ring of weak states which had been created in 1919 out of the ruins of the Habsburg and Romanov empires around her eastern and southern frontiers.

a) France

By 1934 France had long since lost the diplomatic leadership of Europe which she had exercised in the immediate post-war years. Her economy had been belatedly hit by the Depression and her social cohesion threatened by a wave of rioting sparked off in February 1934 by the exposure of a series of financial scandals. Even if she had still possessed the will to intervene militarily in Germany, the Locarno Treaties prevented her from reoccupying the Rhineland. Neither could she rely on Poland after the Polish-German Non-aggression Pact of January 1934. France's response to the new Nazi Germany was therefore hesitant and sometimes contradictory. She sought to contain Germany, as she had done since 1919, through a network of alliances and pacts but, like Britain, she also tried to negotiate with Hitler.

Although ultimately Britain remained France's major European partner, she continued to remain aloof from Continental entanglements until 1939. French alliance policy was therefore primarily aimed at strengthening the Little Entente and negotiating agreements with Italy and Russia. However this was by no means an easy task as in 1933 her relations with both powers were strained. The French were wary of the long-standing Italian ambitions in the Balkans and North Africa and were irritated by Mussolini's tendency to side with the Germans at the Disarmament Conference. Nevertheless, from the summer of 1933 onwards the French launched a major initiative to negotiate an Italian alliance which they believed was crucial in stabilising the Balkans and containing Germany. In the final analysis the French considered Mussolini to be a more important ally than Stalin. They did not therefore reject outright Mussolini's proposal for a four Power pact in May 1933, even though it was aimed at revising the Treaty of Versailles, as they calculated that it might prepare the way for Franco-Italian negotiations. They also hoped to persuade Mussolini to abandon his attempts to destabilise Yugoslavia. Their policy was greatly helped by the abortive Nazi coup in Vienna , which more than anything convinced Mussolini that co-operation with France was essential.

In January 1935 both countries signed the Rome Agreements by which they undertook not to meddle in the affairs of their Balkan neighbours and to act together in the event of unilateral German rearmament or another threat to Austrian independence. Italy's new orientation towards Paris appeared to be confirmed when Britain, France and Italy met at Stresa in April 1935 to condemn German rearmament. While historians have tended to dismiss the Stresa Declarations as mere platitudes, the meeting did nevertheless lead on in June to direct Franco-Italian military staff talks to discuss joint action in the event of a German attack on Austria, Italy or France.

Parallel to these negotiations talks were proceeding between the French and the Russians. Paris did not show the same enthusiasm for a Russian alliance as she did for one with Italy. This was partly because Soviet Russia had been regarded as scarcely less of a threat to the West than Germany and partly because Russia no longer had a common border with Germany. In November 1932 the French government had signed a non-aggression pact with Russia, but when in the summer of 1933 the Russians proposed a more ambitious 'secret verbal agreement' on political co-operation, the first reaction of the French was to question Russia's motives. Paul-Boncour, the French Foreign Minister, observed:

> By appearing ... to consider only Germany, and the pursuit of European agreements which would be likely to coincide with our views, is not the USSR really concerned most of all with Japan and prompted by the ulterior motive of committing us in Asia?

Nevertheless, there were compelling reasons to respond positively to Russia's initiatives as the French ambassador in Moscow reminded his government in September 1933

> 1 After a failure of the British and American agreements of the Treaty of Versailles and the creation of equilibrium by the Protocol of 1924, in the middle of the difficulties in which the British Empire and the United States are struggling, which make concrete
> 5 undertakings with regard to European affairs more and more unlikely, this is ... a system based on agreement with the USSR ... which in present circumstances, may guarantee French security.

By April 1934, after the shock of the German-Polish Non-aggression Pact, the French were ready to renew negotiations with Russia. However, they aimed to enmesh Soviet Russia in an elaborate 'treaty of regional assistance' or an 'eastern Locarno' which would be signed not only by Russia but also by Germany, Poland, Czechoslovakia and the

Baltic States. This was to be buttressed by a separate Franco-Russian agreement associating Russia with the 'western' Locarno treaty and France with the proposed eastern pact. But the whole ingenious plan came to nothing as both Germany and Poland refused to join. The Poles were more suspicious of the Russians than of the Germans. France had therefore little option but to pursue a mutual assistance pact with Soviet Russia alone. The final impetus to its negotiation was given by Germany's introduction of conscription in March 1935. By May the Pact had been signed. Even then the French did not quite overcome their suspicions of Soviet Russia. They refused outright to complement the pact with military staff talks. For them it was sufficient that the pact should restrain Russia from moving closer to Germany again as she had done in 1922 when she had signed the Rapallo Agreement (see page 48).

Meanwhile the French government attempted to complement its alliance policy by negotiating a settlement with Germany. Both in the winter of 1933-4 and in the summer of 1935, immediately after the signature of the Franco-Soviet Treaty, attempts were made to open up a Franco-German dialogue. These efforts were doomed as the French attempted to draw the Germans into negotiating agreements essentially aimed at preserving the Versailles system. Hitler was ready, when it suited him, to lower the political temperature through cordial diplomatic exchanges, but he was not ready to tolerate the restrictions with which French - and British - diplomacy was attempting to entangle him.

b) Great Britain

The British government had no illusions about the potential danger from Germany. As early as 1934 Neville Chamberlain, then Chancellor of the Exchequer, described Germany as the '*fons et origo* [fount and origin] of all our European troubles and anxieties'. Like France, Britain's reaction to Nazi Germany was conditioned by her military, economic and strategic vulnerability. In 1933 she faced not only a growing threat from Germany in Europe, but also from Japan in the Far East. By the autumn of 1935 when Italy invaded Abyssinia, this danger was further compounded by possible threats from Italian naval forces to her Mediterranean position. That year the Government's Defence Requirement Committee warned that:

> 1 it is a cardinal requirement of our national and imperial security that our foreign policy should be conducted so as to avoid the possible development of a situation in which we might be confronted simultaneously with the hostility of Japan in the Far
> 5 East, Germany in the West and any power on the main line of communication between the two.

Consequently, the main aim of British policy towards Germany was to blunt Hitler's aggression by continuing to modify the Treaty of Versailles while simultaneously drawing Germany back into the League where she could be enmeshed in multi-lateral agreements on security. Sir John Simon summed up this policy in a letter to King George V in February 1935:

> 1 ... the practical choice is between a Germany which continues to rearm without any regulation or agreement and a Germany which through getting a recognition of its rights and some modification of the Peace Treaties, enters into the comity of nations and
> 5 contributes, in this and other ways, to European stability.

Britain supported any initiative which appeared to lead to the pacification of Europe within the overall structure created by the peace treaties of 1919-20, such as Mussolini's proposal for a four-power pact in 1933, the French plans for an eastern Locarno or the German Polish Non-aggression Treaty, which the Foreign Office believed thawed the 'cold war' that had bedevilled relations between Warsaw and Berlin since 1919. It also worked hard for an overall settlement with Germany. Despite the reintroduction of German conscription in March, Sir John Simon went to Berlin later in the month to explore the possibility of a comprehensive settlement with Germany involving German recognition of Austrian independence, her participation in an 'eastern' Locarno and return to the League. British ministers attended the Stresa meeting on 8 April, but they were determined not to be manoeuvred into an anti-German front. In the Cabinet on 8 April

> 1 ... A suggestion was very generally supported that, if asked by France and Italy to put an end to conversations with Germany and to do nothing more than indicate our intention to stand firm with France and Italy, we should not agree to it ... Our line, therefore, it
> 5 was suggested, should be that we could not agree to make a complete breach with Germany, and to take no action to threaten her ...

The British government was not at that stage ready to join any alliances or pacts directed against Germany as it was convinced that the pre-war alliance system had been a major cause of the very war it was aimed to prevent. In June this policy seemed to be rewarded with success when the Anglo-German Naval Agreement was signed.

Since 1940 appeasement has generally been branded as a weak and ineffectual policy. In many ways, however, it was a realistic policy based on the need of a vulnerable empire to compromise with its potential enemies. Yet ultimately if Germany did not accept her place within a modified framework of the European and world system created by the peace treaties of 1919-20, Britain was eventually prepared to fight to preserve the advantageous position she enjoyed within it. This was to become much clearer after the Munich crisis of September 1938.

c) Italy

Mussolini, who had his own extensive revisionist and imperialist programme which he intended to implement in the Balkans and North Africa, at first attempted to maintain a special position as mediator between Germany on the one hand and Britain and France on the other. He thus hoped that his proposed Four-Power Pact of June 1933 (see page 88) would enable Italy to play a major part in Europe and take a lead in revising those parts of the Treaty of Versailles it disliked. However French scepticism towards the Pact and the increasing German threat to Austria began to convert Mussolini from a critic and potential revisionist of the Treaty of Versailles to an upholder of the territorial status quo. As early as August 1933 Mussolini met Dollfuss, the Austrian Chancellor, at Rimini and discussed arrangements for Italian military support in case of German intervention in Austria. In March 1934 he further strengthened his position against Germany by negotiating the Rome Protocols with Austria and Hungary which provided for diplomatic consultations should any of the three Powers call for them. Mussolini's conversion to a pillar of the existing order was accelerated by the abortive Nazi putsch in Vienna in July 1934 and by the German announcement of conscription the following March. The Rome Agreements of January 1935 were, as we have seen, a triumph for French policy, but they were also significant because they marked France's recognition of Italy as a Great Power in its own right. Mussolini attempted to fulfil this role by taking the lead in orchestrating opposition to German rearmament when he invited Britain and France to the Stresa Conference in April 1935. By the spring of 1935, therefore, Italy appeared to have aligned herself firmly with Britain and France in their desire to preserve - albeit modified in some respects - the Versailles settlement.

d) Soviet Russia

Like Mussolini, but for different reasons, Stalin was becoming increasingly conservative in his approach to foreign policy issues and was ever more anxious to preserve the status quo. This was not only because Russia was threatened in the Far East by Japan, but also because she was particularly vulnerable to attack while she was involved through the collectivisation programme in an immense internal upheaval. Stalin, like the other European leaders, reacted cautiously to the Nazi take over of power. He was not sure how long Hitler would remain as chancellor. In 1930 he had ordered the German Communist Party not to co-operate with the Socialists on the grounds that a victory of the Nazis, whom he thought were the puppets of the great industrialists, would lead to a German Communist revolution. Even if this were not to happen, he hoped that the traditions of the Rapallo policy and a common hatred of Poland would ensure the continuation of Soviet-German co-operation. His distrust of the West was at least as great as his fear of Nazi Germany. At the seventeenth congress of the Russian Communist Party in 1934 he observed:

> 1 Some politicians say that the USSR has now taken an orientation towards France and Poland; that from an opponent of the Versailles Treaty it has become a supporter of that treaty, and that this change is to be explained by the establishment of the Fascist
> 5 regime in Germany. That is not true. Of course, we are far from being enthusiastic about the Fascist regime in Germany. But Fascism is not the issue here, if only for the reason that Fascism in Italy, for instance, has not prevented the USSR from establishing the best relations with that country.

Stalin, like the French and British governments, tried both to strengthen his defences against Germany and to appease Hitler. Whilst discussing possible security pacts with the French and joining the League of Nations in September 1934, he attempted to maintain good relations with Germany despite such setbacks as the German-Polish Non-aggression Pact. In 1934, for instance, Russia repaid most of the loans it had borrowed from Germany and proposed to Hitler a joint agreement guaranteeing the independence of the Baltic states. The Russian negotiations with the French in the spring of 1935 were also accompanied by a series of secret talks with the Germans, which mirrored the French tactics of trying for a settlement with Hitler in the summer of 1935 as an alternative to the Nazi-Soviet Pact. Soviet-Nazi talks continued intermittently right up to February 1936. Only with the ratification of the Pact by the French parliament were they finally broken off.

e) The United States

In 1933 there was considerable sympathy in America for post-war republican Germany, while both Britain and France were viewed with some suspicion on account of their huge colonial empires. However, Nazi Germany rapidly squandered this reservoir of good will through such ideological actions as the persecution of the Jews. But, in the short term, mounting popular irritation with Nazi Germany was insufficient to influence the foreign policy of the American government, which was determined to keep clear of any European entanglements. Similarly in the Far East the United States was alarmed by the Japanese occupation of Manchuria, but did no more than make diplomatic protests. Indeed, the Temporary Neutrality Act of 1935, by empowering the President to ban the supply of arms to all belligerents - whether aggressors or victims of aggression - in the event of the outbreak of war, strengthened this policy of non-involvement.

5 The Abyssinian Crisis

Mussolini had for a long time wanted to build up an impressive empire in North Africa which would have the added advantage of distracting his people from the impact of the Depression on the Italian economy. By 1932 he had begun to plan in earnest the annexation of Abyssinia. Not only would Abyssinia provide land for Italian settlers, but it would also connect Eritrea with Italian Somaliland and thus put most of the Horn of Africa under Italian control. In December 1934 a clash occurred between Italian and Abyssinian troops at the small oasis of Wal-Wal some 50 miles on the Abyssinian side of the border with Italian Somaliland. The following October the long expected invasion of Abyssinia began. Mussolini was convinced that neither Britain nor France would raise serious objections. In January 1935 Laval, the French Foreign Minister, had verbally promised him a free hand, while

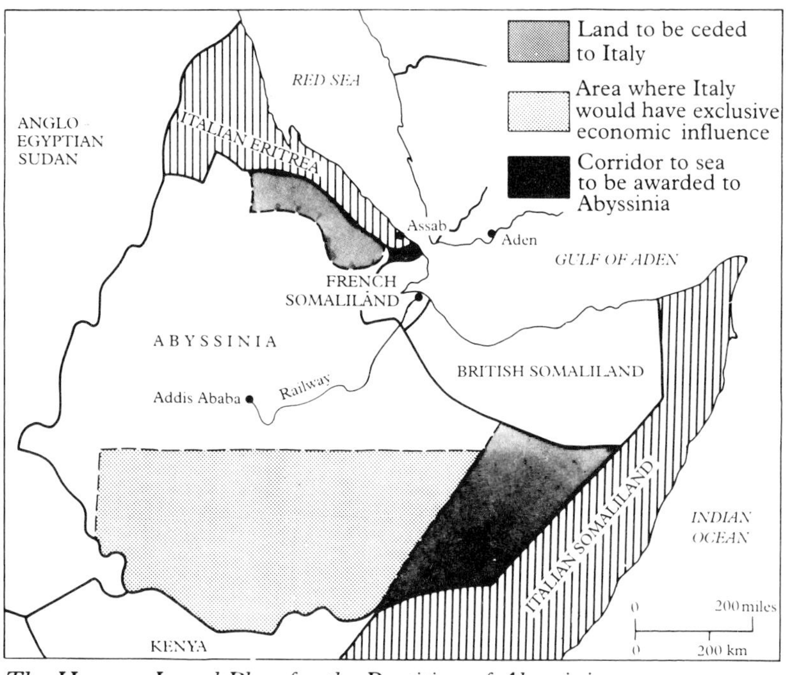

The Hoare – Laval Plan for the Partition of Abyssinia

the British Foreign Office was desperate to avert the crisis either by offering Mussolini territorial compensation elsewhere or by helping to negotiate an arrangement, comparable to Britain's own position in Egypt, which would give Italy effective control of Abyssinia without formal annexation. Sir Robert Vansittart, a senior British diplomat, forcefully pointed out that:

> 1 The position is as plain as a pikestaff. Italy will have to be bought off - let us use and face ugly words - in some form or other, or Abyssinia will eventually perish. That might in itself matter less, if it did not mean that the League would also perish (and that Italy
> 5 would simultaneously perform another volte-face into the arms of Germany ...)

Why then could such a compromise not be negotiated? The scale and brutality of the Italian invasion confronted both the British and French governments with a considerable dilemma. The British government was facing an election in November 1935 and was under intense pressure from the electorate to support the League. In an unofficial peace ballot organised by the League of Nations Union in June 1935, 10 out of 11 million replies backed the use of economic sanctions by the League in a case of aggression. In France public opinion was more divided with the Left supporting the League and the Right supporting Italy. However, both Powers feared the diplomatic consequences of alienating Italy over Abyssinia. In particular, Britain's persistent refusal to join France in guaranteeing the status quo in central and eastern Europe inevitably increased the importance for the French of their rapprochement with Italy.

On 18 October the League condemned Italian action and voted for a gradually escalating programme of sanctions. In the meantime both Britain and France continued to search for a compromise settlement. In December Laval and the British Foreign Minister, Sir Samuel Hoare, produced a plan which had in fact already been discussed by the League in September. It involved effectively placing some two thirds of Abyssinia under Italian control. There was a strong possibility that it would have been acceptable to Mussolini, but it was leaked to the French press and an explosion of rage amongst the British public forced Hoare's resignation and the dropping of the plan. The failure of diplomacy did not then ensure vigorous action against Mussolini. The League put no embargo on oil exports to Italy, and Britain refused to close the Suez Canal to Italian shipping on the grounds that this might lead to war. Mussolini was thus able to step up his campaign and by May had overrun Abyssinia.

Britain and France had gained the worst of all worlds. They had alienated Italy and failed to deter future aggressors by using the League as an effective institution for enforcing collective security. The only

Power to benefit immediately from the crisis was Germany. In this sense the Abyssinian crisis rather than the Manchurian crisis was indeed the crucial turning point in the 1930s. Not only did it irreparably weaken the League and provide Hitler with an ideal opportunity for the illegal remilitarisation of the Rhineland, but it also effectively destroyed the Franco-Italian rapprochement and ultimately replaced it with the Rome-Berlin 'Axis'. This eventually enabled Hitler in 1938 to absorb Austria without Italian opposition. The 'Axis' was also to threaten vital British and French lines of communication in the Mediterranean with the possibility of hostile naval action and thus seriously weaken their potential response to future German - or indeed Japanese- aggression.

6 The Remilitarisation of the Rhineland

The remilitarisation of the Rhineland marked an important stage in Hitler's plans for rebuilding German power. With the construction of strong fortifications there he would be able to counter any French attempts to come to the rescue of their eastern allies. Hitler had originally planned to make a move in 1937, but a combination of the favourable diplomatic situation created by the Abyssinian crisis and the need to distract domestic attention from German economic problems brought about by the speed of the rearmament programme, persuaded him to act in March 1936. In December 1935 the German Army was ordered to start planning the reoccupation, while Hitler's diplomats began to manufacture a legal justification for such action by arguing that the Franco-Soviet Pact was contrary to the Locarno Agreement. Crucial to the success of his plan was the attitude of Italy. Mussolini, isolated from the other Stresa Powers because of his Abyssinian policy, had little option but to reassure Germany that he would not co-operate with the

The Girls He Left Behind, David Low cartoon

British and French to enforce Locarno if German troops entered the Rhineland.

German troops marched into the Rhineland on 7 March 1936. In order to reassure France that they did not intend to violate the frontier they were initially, at any rate, few in number and lightly equipped. Why then did the French army not immediately intervene? The French General Staff, which since the late 1920s had been planning for a defensive war against Germany based on the fortifications of the Maginot line, refused to invade the Rhineland unless they had full backing from the British. The most the British government was ready to do was to promise France that in the event of an unprovoked German attack on French territory it would send two divisions of troops across the Channel. Essentially British public opinion was convinced that Hitler was merely walking into 'his own back garden'. Hugh Dalton, the Labour shadow Foreign Secretary, emphasised in the Commons on 26 March that:

> it is only right to say bluntly and frankly that public opinion in this country would not support ... the taking of military sanctions or even of economic sanctions against Germany at this time in order to put German troops out of the Rhineland.

The remilitarisation of the Rhineland was a triumph for Hitler, and, as an internal French Foreign Office memorandum of 12 March 1936 stressed, it marked a decisive shift in power from Paris to Berlin:

> 1 A German success would likewise not fail to encourage elements which, in Yugoslavia, look towards Berlin ... In Rumania this will be a victory of the elements of the Right which have been stirred up by Hitlerite propaganda. All that will remain for Czechoslovakia is
> 5 to come to terms with Germany. Austria does not conceal her anxiety. 'Next time it will be our turn' ... Turkey, who has increasingly close economic relations with Germany, but who politically remains in the Franco-British axis can be induced to modify her line. The Scandinavian countries ... are alarmed.

7 The Spanish Civil War

The civil war in Spain was essentially a domestic matter which rapidly became an international issue threatening to involve the major Powers in a European conflict. It began in July 1936 with a Nationalist revolt led by the army against the Spanish Republican government. When the rebels were defeated in a number of cities by armed workers militias, both sides appealed to the international community for help. The Nationalists, led by General Franco, looked to Germany and Italy, while the Republicans approached Britain, France and Soviet Russia. In 1946 at the Nuremberg trials Göring, who had been the commander of the German Air Force in 1936, recalled Franco's request:

> 1 When the Civil War broke out in Spain ... Franco sent a call for help to Germany and asked for support, particularly in the air. Franco with his troops was stationed in Africa and ... he could not get his troops across, as the fleet was in the hands of the
> 5 Communists ... the decisive factor was, first of all to get his troops to Spain ... The Führer thought the matter over. I urged him to give support under all circumstances; firstly to prevent the further spread of Communism; secondly, to test my young *Luftwaffe* [airforce] in this or that technical aspect.

Hitler quickly agreed to provide a fleet of transport aircraft to fly Franco's men across to Spain. He then followed this up with the dispatch of some 6000 troops. Hitler's motives for providing assistance were probably more complex than Göring indicated. Hitler later claimed that he wanted to distract the western powers so that he could continue to rearm without fear of intervention. He was also aware of the advantages of having a friendly government in Madrid which would not only supply Germany with Spanish mineral resources but would also in wartime possibly provide bases for German submarines. Mussolini after some hesitation, as he had wanted to keep open the option of resurrecting the Stresa Front, agreed to assist Franco for the same mixture of ideological and strategic reasons: he hoped to defeat the Left in Spain, gain a new ally in Franco and 'strengthen' the Italian character by exposure to war.

With both Germany and Italy openly helping Franco there was a real danger of a European war, should France and Britain be drawn in on the Republican side. When the French Prime Minister, Leon Blum, whose power rested on a left-wing coalition was first asked for help by the Republic, he was tempted to send it, if only to deny potential allies of Germany a victory in Spain. However, two factors forced him to have second thoughts. Firstly the actual dispatch of French military aid to the Republicans would have polarised French society which was already deeply divided between Right and Left and run the risk of plunging France into a civil war of its own; and secondly the British government came out strongly against intervention. The British Ambassador in Paris even threatened neutrality should French assistance to the Republicans lead to war with Germany. Despite the strategic dangers for Britain's position in the Mediterranean in the event of a Nationalist victory, the Cabinet viewed the civil war as essentially a side issue, which must not be allowed to prevent its continued search for a lasting settlement with Germany. In addition, there were powerful voices within the Conservative Party, who actively sympathised with Franco.

The Republican government therefore had little option but to approach Soviet Russia for help. In September 1936 Stalin sent hundreds of military advisers and large quantities of military equipment, while the Comintern (the Communist international organisation based in Moscow) was made responsible for recruiting brigades of international volunteers. Stalin, like Hitler, saw the civil war as a way of dividing his enemies. In a bitter attack on the non-intervention policies of Britain and France he in fact described one of the aims of his own policy:

1 There shines through the policy of non-intervention the desire ... to permit all the participants in a war to become deeply bogged down in the mire of the war, to encourage them surreptitiously in this direction, to let them weaken and exhaust each other ... and
5 then when they are sufficiently weakened, to come on to the scene with fresh forces ..., and to dictate one's terms to the weakened participants in the war.

A conflict between the Western Powers and Germany would certainly have suited Stalin's policy, but he was also anxious to prevent a Nationalist victory in Spain since this would strengthen the forces of international Fascism and make a German attack on the Soviet Union more likely.

In an attempt to prevent the war spreading Britain and France proposed a non-intervention agreement. This was signed by the other European Powers, but Germany and Italy ignored it and continued to assist Franco. Stalin likewise went on helping the Republicans, but by early 1937, when he realised that they could not win, he reduced the flow of arms to a level that was just sufficient to prolong the conflict. In this he was successful as it was not until March 1939 that Franco at last occupied Madrid.

For the Democracies the civil war could not have come at a worse time. It polarised public opinion between Right and Left, threatened France with encirclement and cemented the Italian-German rapprochement. It may also have helped to convince the Soviet Union of the weakness of the West and prepared the way for the Nazi-Soviet Pact of September 1939 (see page 120). As with the Abyssinian crisis it was undoubtedly Germany who benefited most from the conflict since it diverted the attention of the Powers during the crucial period 1936-7 from the Nazi rearmament programme.

8 The Diplomatic Revolution, 1936-7: The Rome-Berlin Axis and the Anti-Comintern Pact

The summer of 1936 saw increasingly cordial relations between Berlin and Rome. While Britain pointedly refused to recognise the King of Italy as the 'Emperor of Abyssinia', Germany rapidly did so. Hitler and

Mussolini also co-operated in blocking a new British initiative to up-date the Locarno Treaty. Italy's growing hostility towards Britain, France and especially Russia, with whom until the Spanish Civil War she had enjoyed good relations, also ensured that she had to be more tolerant of German influence in Austria. In January 1936 Mussolini assured the German Ambassador in Rome that

> If Austria, as a formerly independent state, were ... in practice to become a German satellite, he would have no objection.

On 11 July an Austro-German agreement was successfully negotiated on this basis. Germany recognised Austrian independence, while Vienna promised to pursue a German orientated foreign policy and to bring leading Nazis into government. This removed the most contentious issue between Italy and Germany and prepared the way for a German-Italian agreement, the October Protocols, which were signed in Berlin in October 1936. Mussolini announced this new alignment to the world at a mass meeting in Milan on 1 November:

> 1 The Berlin conversations have resulted in an understanding between our two countries over certain problems which have been particularly acute. But these understandings ... this Berlin-Rome line is not a diaphragm but rather an axis around which can revolve
> 5 all those European states with a will to collaboration and peace.

Three weeks later Hitler overrode advice from his professional diplomats and signed the Anti-Comintern Pact with Japan. This was more of symbolic than practical importance as it was aimed against the Communist International (Comintern) rather than the Soviet Union itself. Its value for Japan was that at a time when she was facing increasing hostility from China and Russia in the Far East, she could signal to Moscow that she was no longer isolated. For Hitler, too, coming so soon after the Rome-Berlin Axis, it showed the world that Germany was no longer isolated, as she had appeared to be in the spring of 1935. In November 1937 the Pact was further strengthened by Italy's accession. Britain, France, Russia and even the United States would now have to come to terms with the fact that 'a new globe spanning alliance', as Gerhard Weinberg has described it, was apparently being created which could threaten them simultaneously on both sides of the world. It was now the Democracies and not Germany that were on the defensive.

Making notes on *'The Impact of the Great Depression on International Politics, 1930-6'*

As you re-read this chapter try to identify why and how the Great

Depression helped to weaken the peace settlements and bring to power politicians who were increasingly ready to act unilaterally to defend their countries' interests. Look particularly at the rise of Hitler and the reaction of the Great Powers to his policies.

When you make your notes, concentrate primarily on the following issues:

1. The immediate impact of the Great Depression. Here you need to look particularly at the Manchurian crisis and at Germany, 1930-3.
2. German foreign policy, 1933-6. Ask yourself whether Hitler's policy had any continuities with Brüning's or even Stresemann's policies.
3. The reaction of the Great Powers to the rise of Nazi Germany. Note carefully the impact of the Abyssinian and Spanish Civil Wars on their attempts to create a united front against Germany.

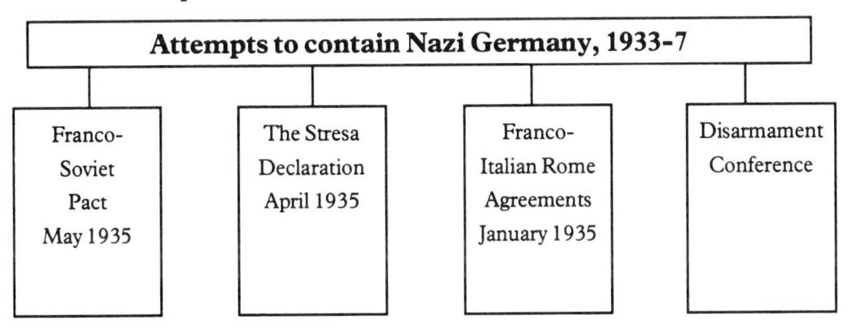

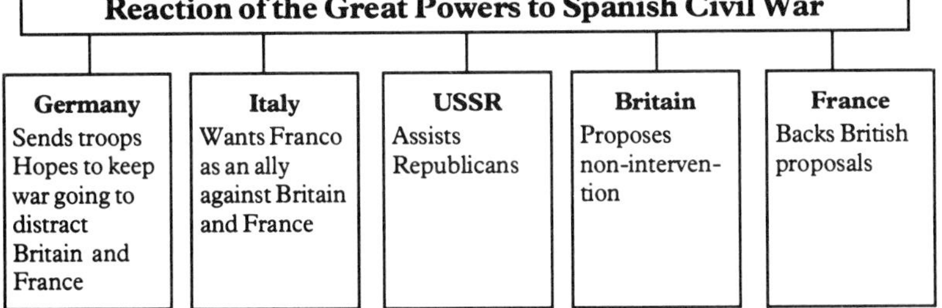

Summary - The Great Depression and International Politics, 1930-6

***Answering essay questions on** The Impact of the Great Depression on International Politics*

The years 1930-7 are an important 'watershed' in the inter-war years. They see the collapse of the League and the Locarno system and the emergence of Nazi Germany. Examiners do frequently set in both outline and special papers questions which are restricted to the years 1930-6, but you should also be ready to deal with more general questions which require you to analyse thematically topics from the early 1920s right up into the 1930s. For instance, if you look at the *Answering Essay Questions* section at the end of chapter 4 (pages 79-80) you will see that some questions set there also relate to the years 1930-6. Question 2 in this section cannot be fully answered without reference to the Depression, the rise of Hitler and the consequences of the Abyssinian crisis. Nor can questions 7 and 8 be properly prepared without a knowledge of the Manchurian and Abyssinian crises. Similarly, questions are often set relating to events from 1930 right up to 1939. These will be discussed in the next chapter. As exam questions do not always neatly fit into text book chapters, it is all the more important to make sure that your notes are methodical and comprehensive. Study the following questions which are a mixture of detailed and more general topics:

1 What were the international consequences of the Great Depression?
2 Account for the collapse of the Versailles and Locarno systems by 1936.
3 Why were the Great Powers so ineffective in containing Hitler, 1933-6?
4 To what extent did Hitler merely follow the policy of his predecessors up to the end of 1936?
5 Compare and contrast the damage done to the League of Nations by the Manchurian and Abyssinian crises.
6 Why did the Spanish Civil War increasingly assume such international significance?

The basic themes underlying questions on the years 1930-6 are the impact of the Great Depression on international relations and the collapse of collective security. The destructive consequences of the Great Depression are explored most directly in the first three questions. Question 1 is the most straightforward, but in answering it you must be careful not to give just an account of events in Manchuria, of Brüning's and Hitler's foreign policy, America's retreat into isolation, etc.,. You must really show *how* the Depression acted as a catalyst for many of these events. Before writing the essay it would be a good idea to draw up a list of the major consequences in order of importance. Questions 2 and

3 are more complicated in that they focus more indirectly on the Depression. In question 2 was it the Depression which brought about the eventual collapse of the Versailles and Locarno systems by bringing Hitler to power? Or were there other factors, such as the traditional reluctance of Britain and America to guarantee French security, operating quite independently of the Depression? In question 3 there is a similar problem: what part did the Depression play in making the efforts of the Great Powers to contain Germany so ineffectual? It would be useful to draw up a list of points backed by evidence showing how the Depression weakened the Democracies, but is this the whole story? How would you for instance evaluate Hitler's own successful attempts to avoid openly challenging the Powers until 1936? Why did Britain and France so mishandle the Abyssinian crisis? Why was the outbreak of the Spanish Civil War good news for Hitler? Question 4 focuses on the question of the continuity of German foreign policy. To answer this you will need to re-read your notes on Stresemann from chapter 4. Then draw up a list of the similarities and differences between the foreign policy of Hitler and his predecessors. It will be particularly important to explore not only their short-term policies but also their ultimate aims. Questions 5 and 6 are of the type which you cannot waffle your way through if you do not know your facts! You can best prepare your answer for question 5 by first drawing up a list of the ways in which each crisis damaged the League. This should also help you then to make the relevant comparisons. How would you go on to plan your essay? Remember that the surest way of writing a poor answer would be just to 'tell the story' first of the Manchurian crisis and then of the Abyssinian crisis. You need to treat the two crises thematically and to keep making contrasts and comparisons right through your essay. Question 6 is a straightforward question once you know your facts! The best way to prepare your answer would be once again to draw up a list of reasons why each Power was affected by the war. It was certainly a war in which three Great Powers did participate to a limited extent, but did it ever cease to be essentially a Spanish struggle?

Source-based questions on *'The Impact of the Great Depression on International Politics'*

1 German Foreign Policy, 1930-6

Carefully read the extracts from *Mein Kampf* on page 87, Bülow's memorandum on pages 88-9 and Hitler's speech on page 89. Answer the following questions.

a) What was the new foreign policy that Hitler was proposing in 1924? (2 marks)
b) Why is Bülow advising Hitler to proceed carefully in 1934? (3 marks)

c) Do these extracts show that Hitler was in reality a cautious politician and that his aim to expand eastwards was just a pipe dream? Explain your answer fully. (10 marks)

2 The Reactions of Britain, France and Russia to Nazi Germany
Read carefully the comments by Paul-Boncour and the French Ambassador on page 91, the statements by Sir John Simon and the Cabinet page 93 and Stalin's speech on page 95. Answer the following questions:

a) Why is Paul-Boncour less enthusiastic about a Franco-Russian alliance than the French Ambassador in Moscow? (5 marks)
b) In what ways might Stalin's statement be seen as strengthening Paul-Boncour's arguments? (5 marks)
c) Read the extracts on pages 91 and 93. Explain fully what differences they show between the British and French reaction to the growing threat from Germany. (5 marks)

3 The Manchurian and Abyssinian Crises, 1931-3 and 1935-6
Carefully read the extracts from the Lytton Commission on page 85, Sir John Simon's speech on page 85, Sir Robert Vansittart's statement on page 97, Hugh Dalton's speech on page 99 and from the French memorandum of 12 March 1936 on page 99. Also look at the cartoon on page 98. Answer the following questions:

a) What does sir John Simon mean when he calls himself 'enough of a pacifist' (line 1)? (2 marks)
b) In what way do the comments by Lord Vansittart and the French Foreign Office help us to understand the point the cartoonist is making? Explain your answer fully. (6 marks)
c) Using these documents and any other evidence known to you examine the view that the Democracies gravely mishandled both the Manchurian and the Abyssinian crises. (12 marks)

4 The Spanish Civil War
Carefully read the statements by Göring and Stalin on pages 100 and 101. Answer the following questions:

a) Why did Göring recommend German assistance for Franco? (3 marks)
b) How accurate was Stalin's assessment of the motives behind the Anglo-French policy of non-intervention? (4 marks)
c) Do these two extracts show that neither Stalin nor Hitler wanted a quick peace in Spain? Explain your answer fully. (8 marks)

CHAPTER 6

The Outbreak of the Second World War

1 Introduction

The diplomatic history of the years 1937-9 is both dramatic and complex. Two of the key Powers made startling U-turns. Nazi Germany, signed a non-aggression pact with Soviet Russia, a state which according to Nazi propaganda was governed by Jews intent on the destruction of Germany and the domination of the world. Similarly Britain abandoned her traditional detachment from Europe and suddenly agreed to guarantee not only Poland but Romania and Greece from attack and ended up fighting a war which she had been determined to avoid. Indeed, all the Great Powers appeared to send out a series of ambiguous and contradictory signals concerning the aims of their foreign policy. This can be more easily understood if it is remembered that the formulation and carrying out of foreign policy is not an exact science. Prime Ministers and Foreign Secretaries may often disagree with each other, as in Britain did Eden and Neville Chamberlain and in France Daladier and Bonnet, and so give conflicting interpretations to apparently agreed policies. Statesmen also may well have long-term aims, but in attempting to realise them they have to be flexible and ready to adapt them to unforeseen events. Bismarck, the unifier of Germany, and one of the great masters of the art of diplomacy, used to keep what were sometimes diametrically opposed options open for as long as possible because he was not sure which approach would ultimately be successful. The statesmen of the late 1930s all followed a similar 'strategy of alternatives', as one historian has described it. Yet beneath this confused manoeuvering their aims are discernible. Britain, France, Russia and America certainly wanted peace but only under conditions that would enable them to survive as independent Great Powers. This meant in practice that Russia would not tolerate unlimited German expansion in eastern Europe, while the western democracies essentially wanted to preserve what was left of the territorial settlements of 1919-23. Germany, Italy and Japan, on the other hand, were determined to carve out new exclusive spheres of influence for themselves respectively in eastern Europe, the Mediterranean and the Far East. By doing this they were all undermining the status quo, which Britain, France and America wished to preserve while the German intention of expanding eastwards directly threatened the security of Soviet Russia.

2 The Outbreak of the Sino-Japanese War

The war in the Pacific which ended with the dropping of atom bombs on

Hiroshima and Nagasaki in 1945 began when a minor incident involving Japanese and Nationalist Chinese troops at the Marco-Polo bridge near Peking on 7 July 1937 rapidly escalated into full-scale hostilities. Japan was determined both to turn northern China into an economic and political satellite and progressively to extend her influence throughout the whole of south-east Asia at the cost of America and the European colonial empires. Inevitably the war emphasised the fragility of British and French power as neither country could afford simultaneous hostilities in Europe and the Far East. Thus as tension mounted in Europe both governments in practice avoided confrontation with the Japanese. In 1937 a senior French diplomat bluntly informed the American ambassador in Paris that:

> 1 ... as long as the present tension existed in Europe it would be impossible for France to take part in any common action in the Far East, which might imply at some stage the furnishing of armed forces ... it was regrettable that this situation existed ... but the
> 5 situation was a fact and had to be faced.

Although America was equally reluctant to take military measures against Japan, the spreading conflict did enable Roosevelt to begin the slow process of re-aligning America with the Democracies against the Axis Powers and Japan. In September 1937 in his famous 'Quarantine Speech' he warned the American people that:

> 1 War is a contagion whether it be declared or undeclared. It can engulf states and peoples remote from the original scene of hostilities. We are determined to keep out of war, yet we cannot insure ourselves against the disastrous effects of war and the
> 5 dangers of involvement.

In December 1937 when British and American ships on the Yangtzee river were attacked by Japanese planes, Roosevelt, despite immediate Japanese apologies and offers of compensation, took the potentially important step of sending an American naval officer to discuss possible future co-operation between the British and American fleets. An American historian, R.G. Utley, has argued that this 'marked the beginning of the alignment of the power of the United States and Britain against the dictator states'. In retrospect this was so, but it was by no means an inevitable process. Chamberlain also had a point when he wrote that 'it is always best and safest to count on nothing from the Americans but words'.

While the Far Eastern War undoubtedly increased the pressure on Britain and France, it did not automatically follow that Japan, Italy and Germany would find it easy to form a common front against the Democracies. The Germans had built up a profitable arms trade with

China and they also feared that Japan might become bogged down in a long war against the Chinese and so in practice become less of a threat to the West. On the other hand, in July 1937 Japan was anxious for diplomatic support from Italy and Germany, but did not want to run the risk of becoming involved in a premature war against Britain and France as a result of a European quarrel. The solution proposed by Berlin that Italy should join Japan in the Anti-Comintern Pact in November 1937 was a clever compromise. It associated Japan with the two Axis Powers in a vague and symbolic pact that was primarily anti-Communist (see page 102), but which potentially could also be directed against the Western Powers as well. Significantly, in the summer of 1939 Japan refused to agree to its conversion into a military alliance, as at a time of mounting tension with Russia she wished to avoid war with Britain and France. Nevertheless, the Pact had considerable political value for Japan. By associating herself with the Axis Powers, she could avoid isolation and play on Franco-British fears of a simultaneous conflict in Europe and the Far East to extract further concessions from them.

3 Hitler Considers his Options

By the autumn of 1937 Hitler had dismantled the Locarno and Versailles systems. The Spanish Civil War and the Sino-Japanese War distracted his potential enemies, while Italy was drawing ever closer to Berlin. In August 1936 he had initiated the Four Year Plan for preparing the German economy for war by 1940. He was thus in a favourable position to consider options for a new and more aggressive phase of foreign policy. Some historians like T. Mason argue that Hitler in reality had no alternative but to go to war. His over-rapid rearmament programme, which was to a great extent dependent on foreign imports, was threatening to plunge the German economy into a major crisis. Only the seizure of new supplies of raw materials, foodstuffs and gold reserves could avert economic collapse. The economy probably was in danger of 'overheating', but, as W. Carr has pointed out it, it is by no means easy to establish that Hitler went to war merely to avoid a developing economic crisis.

On 5 November Hitler called a special meeting which was attended by his Commanders-in-Chief and Foreign and War Ministers. Hitler told them that what he had to say was so important that it was to be regarded as 'his last will and testament'. He then continued:

> 1 The aim of German policy was to make secure and to preserve the racial community and to enlarge it. It was therefore a question of space ... [*Lebensraum*]
> The question for Germany was: Where could she achieve the
> 5 greatest gain at the lowest cost? German policy had to reckon with

two hate inspired antagonists, Britain and France, to whom a German colossus in the centre of Europe was a thorn in the flesh ... Germany's problem could only be solved by the use of force ... If the resort to force with its attendant risks is accepted ... there then
10 remains still to be answered the questions 'When'? and 'How'? In this matter there were three contingencies to be dealt with:
Contingency 1: Period 1943-5
After that date only a change for the worse, from our point of view, could be expected ... Our relative strength would decrease in
15 relation to the rearmament, which would then have been carried out by the rest of the world. If we did not act by 1943-5 any year could, owing to lack of reserves produce the food crisis ... and this must be regarded as a 'waning point of the regime'... If the Führer was still living, it was his unalterable determination to solve
20 Germany's problem of space by 1943-5 at the latest ...
Contingency 2
If internal strife in France should develop into such a domestic crisis as to absorb the French army completely and render it incapable of use for war against Germany, then the time for action
25 against the Czechs would have come.
Contingency 3
If France should be so embroiled in war with another state that she could not 'proceed' against Germany. For the improvement of our politico-military position our first objective, in the event of our
30 being embroiled in war, must be to overthrow Czechoslovakia and Austria simultaneously in order to remove the threat to our flank in any possible operation against the West ...

In a brilliant analysis A.J.P. Taylor has shown that this document, which was compiled by Hitler's adjutant, Colonel Hossbach some five days after the meeting, is in fact a fragment of a copy of the original that has disappeared. Moreover, the meeting it records was in fact not primarily concerned with the aims of foreign policy but with the allocation of armaments between the German armed services. The document has therefore lost some of the significance which was attributed to it when it was used by the Prosecution at the Nuremberg War Crimes Trials in 1946. However, few historians agree with Taylor's conclusions that Hitler's exposition was for the most part 'day dreaming unrelated to what followed in real life' and that he was in fact 'at a loss what to do next even after he had the power to do it'. The consensus of research still decisively favours W. Carr's view that Hitler was warning his generals 'that a more adventurous and dangerous foreign policy was imminent'. As you read this chapter you must make up your own mind about the significance of the *'Hossbach Memorandum'*.

4 Britain, France and Appeasement

In the 20 years after the defeat of Hitler historians tended to take their cue from Winston Churchill's memoirs and dismiss the unheroic attempts of the British and French governments of the time to avert war through negotiation and appeasement as misguided or even cowardly.

Neville Chamberlain became a scapegoat not only for his own countrymen but also for the French and the Germans. French historians and politicians claimed that he bullied them into appeasement, while some Germans were tempted to excuse their own support for Hitler by blaming Chamberlain for not standing up to the Nazis. Only with the opening up of the British and French archives in the 1960s and 1970s did it gradually become possible to reassess the whole policy of appeasement. Now historians see appeasement as 'a central episode in [Britain's] protracted retreat from an untenable world power status' (Robbins) and as an unavoidable consequence of her economic and military weakness.

France was in a similar position to Britain. She, too, was threatened in the Mediterranean by Italy and in the Far East by Japan. Her economy, however, was much weaker than Britain's. Between 1936 and 1938 the franc had to be devalued three times to help pay for rearmament. By 1937 France was dependent on Britain not only economically but also politically. French society was deeply divided as the Right wanted to negotiate with Hitler and Mussolini, while the Left wanted to fight and looked to Russia as an ally. It has been argued that only by allowing Britain to take the lead in negotiating with Germany, and therefore the blame for difficult decisions and possible failures, could French politicians preserve the semblance of social unity in their country. It is not surprising therefore that it was left to Chamberlain, who became Prime Minister in May 1937, to give appeasement its real momentum.

Chamberlain aimed first to repair Anglo-Italian relations with the intention of encouraging Mussolini to restrain Hitler, but opposition from his Foreign Secretary, Anthony Eden, delayed talks until February 1938. In April a preliminary agreement was reached to respect the status quo in the Mediterranean, but it was never implemented because Mussolini did not punctually withdraw his troops from Spain as he had promised to do. Nevertheless, as we shall see, Mussolini did play a crucial moderating role during the Munich crisis in September 1938 and he did remain neutral when war broke out in September 1939. Arguably, however, this was not so much a consequence of Chamberlain's diplomacy but rather of Italy's military and economic weakness.

In the autumn of 1937 Chamberlain launched a major initiative aimed at achieving a settlement with Hitler. Initially, at any rate, appeasement, was a hard-headed attempt to slow up the pace of German expansion in eastern Europe by offering Germany colonies in

Africa, while giving both Britain and France time to accelerate their rearmament programmes. In late November an Anglo-French summit was held in London where this policy was more fully explored. Chamberlain argued:

> 1 It seemed desirable to try to achieve some agreement with Germany on Central Europe whatever might be Germany's aims, even if she wished to absorb some of her neighbours; one could in effect hope to delay the execution of German plans, and even to
> 5 restrain the Reich for such a time that its plans might become impractical in the long run.

Chamberlain won over the French to this policy and by March he was ready to negotiate a package of colonial concessions with Berlin, but the gathering pace of German expansion signalled first by the *Anschluss* and then by the destruction of Czechoslovakia made this approach irrelevant.

5 The *Anschluss* and the Destruction of Czechoslovakia

In November 1937 Hitler had outlined a possible scenario involving civil war in France or a Franco-Italian war (see pages 109-10) which would enable him to annex Austria and dismember Czechoslovakia without fear of international intervention. He was able to achieve these aims in 1938-9 even though the circumstances he predicted never in fact came about. Both the *Anschluss* and the eventual destruction of Czechoslovakia do indeed show Hitler's ability to adapt his tactics to the prevailing circumstances whilst steadily pursuing his overall aims.

a) The *Anschluss*

The annexation of Austria had long been a key aim of Nazi foreign policy, but Hitler did not plan the actual events that enabled him to achieve it. The crisis was ultimately triggered when Schuschnigg, the Austrian Chancellor, alarmed by the activities of the Austrian Nazis, requested an interview with Hitler. Hitler welcomed the chance to achieve an easy diplomatic success by imposing on Schuschnigg an agreement which would not only have subordinated Austrian foreign policy to Berlin but also have given the Austrian Nazi Party complete freedom. However, Schuschnigg then decided unexpectedly to regain some room for manoeuvre by asking his countrymen to vote in a referendum, which he planned to hold on Sunday 14 March for a 'free and German, independent and social, Christian and united Austria'. The immediate danger for the German government was that if Schuschnigg's appeal was endorsed by a large majority, he would be able to renounce his agreement with Hitler. Confronted by this challenge,

Hitler rapidly dropped his policy of gradual absorption of Austria and not only forced Schuschnigg to cancel the referendum but on 12 March ordered the German army to occupy Austria. Then Hitler decided, apparently on the spur of the moment after a highly successful visit to the Austrian city of Linz where he had attended secondary school as a boy, to incorporate Austria into the *Reich* rather than install a satellite Nazi government in Vienna.

Besides violating the Treaty of Versailles which specifically forbade the union of Germany and Austria, Hitler had used force for the first time against an independent state and put himself in a position from which to threaten Czechoslovakia. Why then did this not bring about a repetition of the Stresa Front that was briefly formed in 1934 against German aggression (see page 89)? Some historians argue that this might have happened had the Anglo-Italian talks started in July 1937 rather than in February 1938, but essentially Mussolini had decided as long ago as 1936 that Austria was a German sphere of interest. Not surprisingly therefore, on 11 March, he backed Hitler's decision to invade Austria. Both Britain and France protested to Berlin but neither had any intention of going to war over Austria. Indeed the French were paralysed by an internal political crisis caused by the resignation of the Chautemps ministry and between 10 and 13

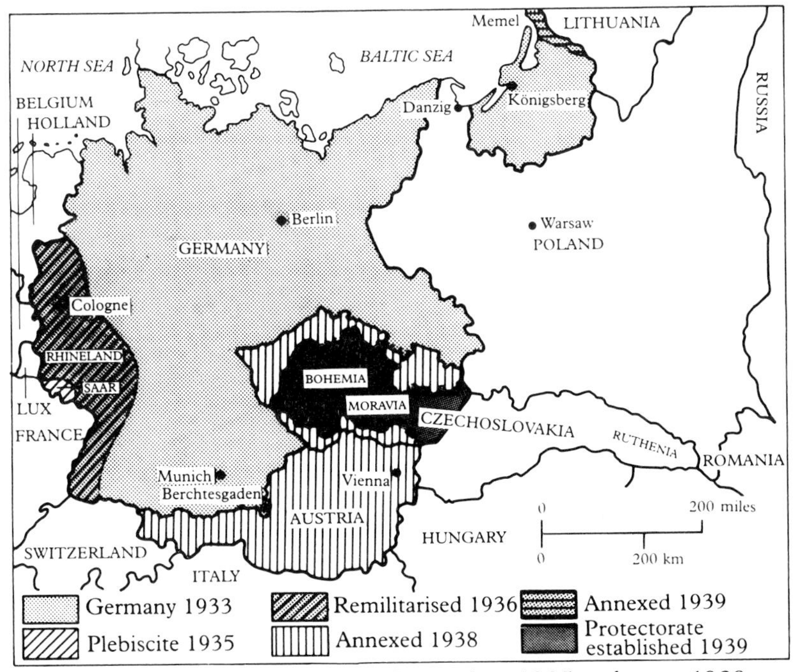

Central Europe showing German Expansion, 1935 – August 1939

March did not even have a government.

The initial reaction of the British government was to hope that the storm would blow over and that talks could resume with Berlin on the package of possible colonial concessions (see pages 111-12) which had already been handed to the German government on 3 March. These concessions were, after all, aimed to distract Berlin from pursuing its ambitions in central Europe. Whether Chamberlain really believed that Hitler could be bought off is hard to say. Privately he wrote that 'it was now perfectly evident that force was the only argument that Germany understood', but publicly he was not yet ready to draw the logical conclusion from this and confront Hitler. Was he gaining time for his country to re-arm or was he seriously giving peace one more chance?

b) The Sudeten Crisis

The annexation of Austria with the minimum of international protest greatly increased the vulnerability of Czechoslovakia to Nazi pressure as she was now surrounded on three sides by German territory. Hitler had long regarded Czechoslovakia, with its alliances with both France and Russia, as a strategic threat to Germany which would eventually have to be eliminated. It is however arguable that in April 1938 Hitler was by no means sure how he was to carry out this aim. He certainly played with the idea of launching a sudden attack on Czechoslovakia if a major crisis were to be triggered, for instance, by the assassination of the German ambassador in Prague. An easier and safer way to bring about the disintegration of Czechoslovakia was to inflame the nationalism of the Sudeten Germans. Czechoslovakia was a fragile state undermined by an ethnically divided population. Its unity was particularly threatened by the three million Sudeten Germans and the two million Slovaks. Hitler therefore specifically instructed Henlein, the Sudeten German leader, to keep making demands for concessions which the Prague government could not possibly grant if it wanted to preserve the unity of Czechoslovakia.

In the aftermath of the *Anschluss* both Britain and France were acutely aware of the growing threat to Czechoslovakia. Britain was unwilling to guarantee Czechoslovakia and yet realised that it might well not be able to stand aloof from the consequences of a German attack upon it. Chamberlain told the Commons on 24 March that if fighting occurred:

> 1 In that event it would be well within the bounds of possibility that other countries, besides those which were parties to the original dispute, would almost immediately become involved. This is especially true in the case of two countries like Great Britain and
> 5 France, with long associations of friendship, with interests closely interwoven, devoted to the same ideals of democratic liberty and determined to uphold them.

The French, unlike the British, were pledged by two treaties signed with Czechoslovakia in 1924 and 1925 to consult and assist in the event of a threat to their common interests. In reality the French were in no position to assist the Czechs. The Chief of the French Air Staff made no secret of his fears that the French air force would be wiped out within 15 days after the outbreak of war with Germany. The French were therefore ready to follow the British lead in seeking a way of defusing the Sudeten crisis before it could lead to war.

The urgency of this was underlined by the war scare of the weekend of 20-21 May when the Czech government suddenly partially mobilised its army in response to false rumours that a German attack was imminent. Hitler, warned by both Britain and France of the dangerous consequences of any military action, rapidly proclaimed the absence of any mobilisation plans. Far from making Hitler more reasonable this incident appears to have had the opposite effect, as he immediately stepped up military preparations for an invasion and set 1 October as a deadline for 'smashing Czechoslovakia'. Taylor sees this as bluff and argues that 'Hitler did not need to act. Others would do his work for him'. There were certainly, as we have seen, powerful forces working for the disintegration of the Czech state, but most historians do not dismiss Hitler's plans so lightly. It is more likely that he was just keeping his options open, as Bullock argues, 'to the very last possible moment'.

Meanwhile, France and Britain were redoubling their efforts to find a peaceful solution. The Anglo-French peace strategy aimed to put pressure on both the Czechs and the Sudeten Germans to make concessions, while continuing to warn Hitler of the dangers of a general war. In early September Benes, the Czech Prime Minister, responded to this pressure by granting almost all Henlein's demands. As this threatened the justification for Hitler's campaign against Czechoslovakia, Hitler immediately instructed Henlein to provoke a series of incidents which would enable him to break off the talks with Benes.

On 12 September Hitler's campaign moved into a new phase when in a speech at the Nuremberg rally he violently attacked the Czechs and assured the Sudetens of his support. Both Britain and France desperately attempted to avoid war. Daladier, the French Prime Minister, suggested that he and Chamberlain should meet Hitler, but Chamberlain seized the initiative and flew to see Hitler on 15 September at Berchtesgaden. There he agreed, subject to consultation with the French, that Czechoslovakia should cede to Germany all areas which contained a German population of 50 per cent or over. This would be supervised by an international commission. Hitler also demanded that Czechoslovakia should renounce her pact with Soviet Russia. When Chamberlain again met Hitler at Bad Godesberg on 22 September after winning French backing for his plan, Hitler demanded that the German occupation of the Sudetenland should be speeded up so that it would be completed by 28 September. Nor was it to be supervised by any international commission. Why Hitler should suddenly have changed his mind has puzzled historians. Taylor argued that Hitler was anxious to avoid accepting Chamberlain's plan in the hope that the Hungarians and Poles would formulate their own demands for Czechoslovakian territory and that he would then be able to move in and occupy the whole state under the pretext of being 'a peace-maker' creating a 'new order'. On the other hand it is possible that Hitler had no such elaborate plan in mind and merely wanted to eliminate Czechoslovakia once and for all through war. At this stage Chamberlain's peace initiative seemed to have failed. France and Britain reluctantly began to mobilise, although both Powers still continued to seek a negotiated settlement. In retrospect it is often argued that they should have gone to war and called Hitler's bluff. Chamberlain's critics particularly stress that Russia was ready to come to the help of Czechoslovakia, but at the time offers of Russian help seemed to the British, French and even the Czechs to be unconvincing. As neither Poland nor Romania would allow Russian troops through their territory how could they help Czechoslovakia? It is thus not surprising that Chamberlain and Daladier warmly welcomed Mussolini's last minute proposal on 28 September for a four Power conference in Munich.The next day reluctantly, under pressure from his generals and Mussolini who both dreaded a premature war, Hitler agreed to delay the occupation of the Sudetenland until 10 October and to allow an international commission to map the boundary line. He also consented, together with Britain, France and Italy, eventually to guarantee what remained of the independence of Czechslovakia and signed a declaration which affirmed the desire of Britain and Germany 'never to go to war with one another again'. This was supplemented by a similar declaration signed by Ribbentrop, Hitler's Foreign Minister, in Paris in December.

It is too simple to call Munich a triumph for Hitler. He had, it is true, secured the Sudetenland, but arguably he had been cheated of his real aim, the destruction of Czechoslovakia, which apparently was now about to be protected by an international guarantee. Germany seemed to be in danger of being enmeshed in just the sort of international agreement Hitler had always hoped to avoid. However, even the most revisionist of historians would be hard put to call Munich a great victory for Chamberlain. It may be that Roy Douglas is right that 'he did about as well as anybody could have done', and arguably he did buy more time for rearmament, but to the outside world Munich seemed to be a major defeat for Britain and France. The British ambassador in Tokyo reported:

> The Japanese reaction ... is that we are prepared to put up with almost any indignity rather than fight. The result is that all in all, our prestige is at a low ebb in the East ...

c) The Destruction of Czechoslovakia

The argument that Hitler merely responded to events is hard to sustain when his foreign policy from October 1938 to March 1939 is analysed. His main priority remained the destruction of Czechoslovakia. On 21 October the German army was ordered to draw up fresh plans for military action. Simultaneously Hitler dangled the bait of territorial gains at the expense of the Czechs in front of the Hungarians, Poles and Romanians in order to enlist their support. German agents were also sent into Slovakia to fuel agitation against Prague. In practice Britain and France were already beginning to recognise Czechoslovakia as a German sphere of influence. The German representatives were allowed to dominate the international commission that was to map out the new frontiers after the secession of the Sudetenland and neither Power protested when Germany refused to participate in finalising the terms of the joint guarantee of Czechoslovakia in February 1939.

On 6 March the Germans were given the opportunity finally to dismember Czechoslovakia. When the Czechs suddenly moved troops into Slovakia to crush local demands for independence, which the Nazis, of course had helped stir up, Hitler persuaded the Slovaks to appeal to Berlin for assistance. On 14 March 1939 the Czech President, Hacha, was ordered to travel to Berlin where he was ruthlessly bullied into resigning the fate of his country into 'the hands of the Führer'. The next day German troops occupied Prague, and Slovakia was turned into a German protectorate. This action was to precipitate a major diplomatic revolution in Europe.

6 The Anglo-French Guarantees and Attempts to Construct a Peace Front

In 1925 the British Foreign Minister had declared that the defence of the Polish Corridor was not worth the bones of one British grenadier, yet on 30 March 1939 Britain broke decisively with her traditional foreign policy of avoiding a Continental commitment and guaranteed Poland against a German attack. In many ways it appeared a foolhardy and contradictory gesture as both Britain and France lacked the military power to defend Poland and had already tacitly written off eastern Europe as a German sphere of influence. What caused this U-turn was the speed and brutality of the German occupation of the Czech province of Bohemia, which clearly indicated that Hitler could no longer be trusted to respect treaties and guarantees. It is also important to stress that, in the spring of 1939, the French economy and with it French self-confidence had made a strong recovery. Thus a tougher policy towards Hitler increasingly appeared to the French government to be a realistic option.

Britain was initially stampeded into this revolutionary new policy by panic-striken rumours on 17 March that Hitler was about to occupy Romania and seize the oil wells there. Access to these would greatly strengthen the German war industry and enable it to survive any future British naval blockade. At first Britain aimed to contain Germany by negotiating a four power pact with France, Russia and Poland, but given the intense suspicion with which Russia was viewed by Poland and the other eastern European states this was not a practical policy. Yet when Hitler went on to force Lithuania to hand back the former German city of Memel to the Reich on 23 March, it became even more vital to deter Hitler by any means possible. Thus Chamberlain and Daladier had little option but to announce on 31 March an immediate Anglo-French guarantee of Poland against external attack. The Polish guarantee was, however, seen as merely the first step towards constructing a comprehensive security system in eastern Europe. Chamberlain hoped to buttress it with a series of inter-locking security pacts with other eastern European and Baltic states.

When, on 7 April, Mussolini invaded Albania a similar wave of panic amongst the eastern Mediterranean states galvanised Britain and France to guarantee both Greece and Romania. In May Britain considerably strengthened her position in the eastern Mediterranean by negotiating a preliminary agreement with Turkey for mutual assistance 'in the event of an act of aggression leading to war in the Mediterranean area'. By July both Bulgaria and Yugoslavia were beginning to gravitate towards the Anglo-French 'peace bloc', but Hitler's success in negotiating an agreement with Soviet Russia on 23 August was to deal a shattering blow to Anglo-French prestige in eastern Europe and the Balkans.

7 The German Break with Poland

At first sight it is puzzling that Hitler should have gone to war with Poland in September 1939. He had, after all, signed a non-aggression pact with her in 1934 and she had helped put pressure on the Czechs during the Munich crisis. By early 1939, however, Polish subservience to Berlin was becoming increasingly vital as Hitler realised that he might have to defeat Britain and France before moving eastwards to secure 'living space' in the Ukraine. In October 1938, and then again in January and March 1939, Hitler and Ribbentrop unsuccessfully sounded out the Poles about the return of Danzig, the construction of a road and rail link through the Corridor and joining the Anti-Commintern Pact. In return the Poles were offered the eventual prospect of acquiring land in the Ukraine. Essentially Hitler wanted to turn Poland into a reliable satellite, but given the fate of Czechoslovakia it was precisely this status that the Poles finally rejected in March 1939. The Anglo-French guarantee of Poland, far from deterring Hitler, convinced him that Poland would have to be eliminated even if this meant war with Britain and France. On 23 May Hitler told his generals:

> 1 Poland will always be on the side of our adversaries ... Danzig is not the objective. It is a matter of expanding our living space in the east ... We cannot expect a repetition of Czechoslovakia. There will be fighting. The task is to isolate Poland ... Basic principle: conflict
> 5 with Poland, beginning with the attack on Poland, will be successful only if the West keeps out. If that is impossible, then it is better to attack the West and finish off Poland at the same time. It will be a task of dextrous diplomacy to isolate Poland ...

8 The Russian Factor

Diplomatically the Nazi-Soviet Pact was a revolutionary event as significant as the British guarantee of Poland. To most contemporaries it seemed scarcely credible that Hitler could negotiate an agreement with a power which he was committed to destroy. Yet in retrospect the Nazi-Soviet Pact seems almost inevitable. There were considerable advantages for Stalin in an agreement with Hitler which would keep the Soviet Union out of a war in Europe at a time when Soviet troops were fighting increasingly bitter frontier engagements against the Japanese along the Manchurian and Outer Mongolian borders. Also the prospect of Britain, Germany and France fighting themselves to a standstill in western Europe would not only relieve the pressure on Russia, but improve the prospects for the spread of Communism - Stalin, like the British and Americans, had of course no idea that France would be defeated in six weeks in 1940. For Hitler, once war against Poland seemed inevitable, it was the obvious move that any 'dextrous' diplomat would make. As soon as victory was assured over Poland and the Western Democracies, Soviet Russia could then be dealt with.

The Anglo-French guarantee of Poland enormously strengthened Stalin's position. To build up their 'peace front' against Hitler the British and French needed a pact with Russia, but now that they were pledged to defend Poland, which was also a barrier against German expansion eastwards, Stalin could afford to play off Hitler against Chamberlain and Daladier. Negotiations between Russia, Britain and France began in April 1939. They were protracted and bedeviled by mutual mistrust. Stalin's demand that Russia should have the right militarily to intervene in the affairs of the small states on her western borders if they were threatened with internal subversion by the Nazis, as Austria and Czechoslovakia were in 1938, was rejected outright by the British. They feared that the Russians would use the threat of Nazi indirect aggression as an excuse to seize the territories for themselves. Stalin on the other hand, was equally suspicious that the Democracies were attempting to manoeuvre the Russians into a position where they would have to do most of the fighting against Germany. The British delegate, William Strang, reported:

> if we do not trust them they equally do not trust us. They are not fundamentally, a friendly power; but they like us, are driven to this course by force of necessity. If we are of two minds about the wisdom of what we are doing, so are they.

The Russians thus had ample time to explore the possibility of a pact with Germany, which became genuinely interested in negotiations once the decision was taken on 23 May to prepare for war against Poland. Right through to the middle of August Moscow continued to keep both options open, but by then the slow pace of Anglo-French-Soviet military discussions seems finally to have convinced Stalin that an agreement with Hitler would be preferable. With only days to go before the start of the military campaign against Poland Hitler was ready to accept Stalin's terms and the Soviet-Nazi pact was signed on 23 August. Not only did the pact commit both Powers to benevolent neutrality towards each other, but in a secret protocol it outlined the German and Russian spheres of interest in eastern Europe: the Baltic states and Bessarabia in Romania fell within the Russian sphere, while Poland was to be divided

Wonder How Long the Honeymoon Will Last? Washington Star, *9 Oct. 1939*

between the two Powers. Above all, by neutralising Soviet Russia the Pact made an attack on Poland a much less risky policy for Hitler, even if Britain and France did try to come to her rescue.

Given the deep and not entirely unjustified suspicions of Soviet Russia in Britain, France and the eastern European states, the Nazi-Soviet Pact was the most likely outcome from the tangle of negotiations that took place in the summer of 1939. It did, however, make a German attack on Poland almost inevitable.

9 The Outbreak of War

On 22 August on the eve of the signature of the Nazi-Soviet Pact Hitler boasted that

> 1 ... To be sure a new situation has arisen. I experienced those poor worms Daladier and Chamberlain in Munich. They will be too cowardly to attack. They won't go beyond a blockade. Against that we have autarchy (self sufficiency) and the Russian raw materials.
> 5 Poland will be depopulated and settled with Germans. My pact with the Poles was merely conceived of as a gaining of time ... After Stalin's death - he is a very sick man - we will break the Soviet Union. Then there will begin the dawn of German rule of the earth.

The omens did indeed look good for Hitler. Although he had failed to convert the Anti-Comintern Pact into a military alliance against Britain and France (see page 109), he had in May concluded the Pact of Steel with Italy by which Mussolini rashly agreed to support Germany militarily. Neither did it appear that appeasement in Britain and France was dead. In June, Lord Halifax stressed that while Britain would defend Poland against any threat to her independence, this did not necessarily mean that her existing frontiers could not be altered or the status of Danzig changed. He went on to repeat a message that was frequently to come out of London in the summer of 1939 - namely that once trust was re-established 'Britain would go far to reach an adjustment with Germany'. In June and July there were also sporadic talks between British and German officials on economic collaboration in Europe and Africa. In France, too, the mood seemed increasingly defeatist. On 15 August the British Embassy reported that 'Bonnet (the French Foreign Minister) was only too ready to discuss a compromise on the Danzig question'.

Overall then Hitler had good grounds to be confident. On 23 August he ordered the army to prepare to attack Poland on the 26th, but then two days later these orders were cancelled because contrary to his expectations Britain had reacted to the news of the Nazi-Soviet Pact by ratifying (or gaining parliamentary approval for) her guarantee of

Poland. Mussolini also announced that he could not fight without impossibly large deliveries of German armaments and equipment. Was there now a chance for a compromise? Superficially it might seem that there was. During the next few days the British and French utilised all the diplomatic channels they could to avoid war, but in the final analysis they were not ready to sacrifice Poland to achieve it. They were unwilling to repeat Munich. They wanted, as Adamthwaite has stressed, 'detente, but negotiated from strength'. Hitler's position was diametrically opposed to this. He was insistent on first destroying Poland and only then negotiating with Britain and France. On 25 August he even offered Britain an alliance and a guarantee of her empire provided she consented to the destruction of Poland and German hegemony in eastern Europe. The response from London continued to be that only after a freely negotiated Polish-German agreement could the future of Anglo-German relations be discussed.

Belatedly it looked as if Hitler was making some concession to this position when, on 29 August, he suddenly demanded that the British should instruct the Poles to send a minister with full negotiating powers to Berlin by the following day. Fearing that Hitler would treat him as he had Schuschnigg and Hacha, the British government refused to press the Poles to go to Berlin, and instead argued that such a deadline was impracticable since time was needed to prepare for negotiations. Was a last minute chance to save the peace lost? Taylor argues that war began simply because Hitler launched 'on 29 August a diplomatic manoeuvre which he ought to have launched on 28 August'. It is more likely, however, that Hitler was aiming to isolate Poland and to manoeuvre her into a position where her 'stubborness' could be blamed for starting the war. Halder, the Chief-of-Staff of the German Army, summarised Hitler's tactics:

> 1 Attack starts September Ist ... Führer will let us know at once if we
> are not to strike ... Führer very calm and clear ... Plan: we demand
> Danzig, corridor through Corridor, and plebiscite on same basis as
> Saar. England will perhaps accept, Poland probably not. Wedge
> 5 between them!

Arguably these demands were relatively moderate, but how genuine were they? All the evidence points to Hitler's determination to destroy Poland. Even if the Poles had turned up in Berlin, the plan according to Halder was:

> Basic principles: raise a barrage of demographic [statistical] and democratic demands ... 30.8. Poles in Berlin. 31.8. Blow up. 1.9. Use of force.

Even when, on 1 September, Germany at last invaded Poland, frantic efforts to avert war still continued. Mussolini urged a Four-Power European Conference, and only when it was absolutely clear that Hitler would not withdraw his troops from Poland did Britain and France declare war on Germany on 3 September.

10 Assessment

The outbreak of the Second World War is arguably the main theme that dominates the events covered in this book. To what extent was it inevitable? Was it essentially a continuation of the First World War or an entirely different conflict which competent diplomacy could have prevented? In 1918 Germany was' beaten but not destroyed'. She still remained potentially strong and ultimately capable of making a second attempt at dominating Europe. In that sense the Treaty of Versailles which humiliated but did not permanently weaken Germany could well be seen as the 'seed bed' of the Second World War. Arguably the chain of crises which started with the *Anschluss* and ended in the German attack on Poland owed its origins to the Versailles settlement. Does it therefore follow that Versailles made war inevitable? Stresemann, Briand and Austen Chamberlain appeared for a time to be able to make the settlement work after modifying the reparation clauses. Nevertheless, it was clear that a revived Germany would still demand its drastic revision, as indeed Stresemann was already beginning to do by the late 1920s. In that sense there was a natural continuity of aims between the Weimar Republic and the Third *Reich*. Yet despite Taylor's attempts to portray Hitler as a normal politician, his seizure of power in January 1933 did make a crucial difference. He gave a new and powerful impetus based on the doctrine of racial superiority to German demands for *Lebensraum* in eastern Europe. The mistake the ex-Allies made was to tolerate Hitler's expansionary policies for so long. When the time came to call a halt, it was no longer possible to do so without a major war.

To a certain extent the horrendous figure of Adolf Hitler obscures the fact that the British and French governments went to war to maintain their position as Great Powers rather than to wage a crusade against the evil force of Nazism. There is no doubt that Hitler's successes in eastern Europe in 1938-9 did threaten to destabilise the whole Continent. After the German occupation of Bohemia the British and French governments believed that they had no choice but to oppose Hitler if they wished to maintain any influence in Europe. Of course they still kept the door open to negotiations, and pursued the will o' the wisp of a general settlement with Germany, but essentially Britain and France were ready to risk war in 1939. Indeed the British Treasury was beginning to argue that Britain's financial position would decline after 1939, and that if war had to come it was preferable sooner rather than later. In France Daladier had steadied the economy and the aeronautical industry was rapidly expanding in early 1939.

It does seem therefore that Britain and France went to war in 1939 as they did in 1914 to contain Germany and safeguard their own Great Power status. Arguably then it was a continuation of the same struggle, even though Italy, Japan and Russia were now potential allies of the Germans. Could it be, however, as Maurice Cowling argues, that Nazi Germany did not in fact threaten Britain and that it was Chamberlain who incurred German hostility by unnecessarily intervening in the Sudeten crises of May and September 1938? The main thrust of Hitler's policy was certainly eastwards, but as early as November 1937, or so the *Hossbach Memorandum* indicates, (see pages 109-10) he was obviously envisaging the possibility of having to fight both the Western Powers. Could genuine British and French independence have survived a German victory in eastern Europe? Would Hitler have tolerated such independence without taking steps to diminish it?

The Road To War

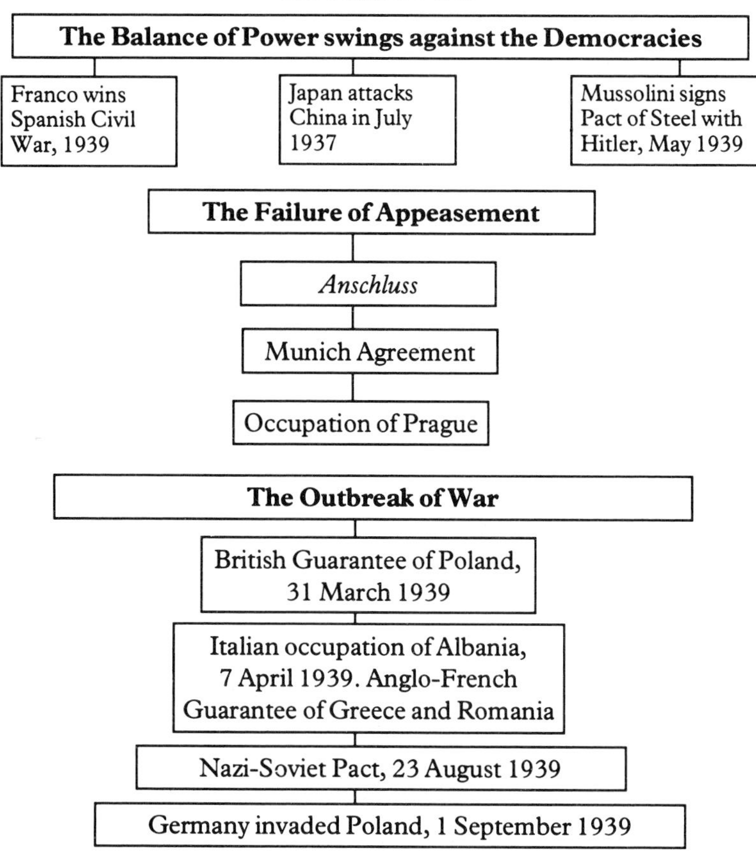

Summary - The Outbreak of the Second World War

Making notes on *'The Outbreak of the Second Word War'*

Your notes on this chapter should be fairly detailed. As you write them up, you should constantly keep these four key questions in mind: i) What were Hitler's aims?; ii) Why did appeasement fail?; iii) Why and how did the Second World War break out?; iv) Why could Britain and France no longer count on the support of Italy, Japan and Russia? Careful and detailed answers to the following problems should provide you with a relevant framework for your notes:

1 What were the international consequences of the Sino-Japanese War up to September 1939?
2 How helpful is the *Hossbach Memorandum* as a guide to Hitler's aims?
3 To what extent did Hitler plan the *Anschluss,* the annexation of the Sudetenland and the occupation of Prague or was he taking advantage of a favourable situation?
4 Why did Britain and France appear to tolerate these annexations and yet decide on 31 March to guarantee Poland?
5 Why did Stalin sign the Nazi-Soviet Pact and not an alliance with Britain and France?
6 Conclusion: Could the German attack on Poland have been avoided? Was the Second World War unavoidable?

Answering essay questions on *'The Outbreak of the Second World War'*

Since the causes of the Second World War are one of the most obvious and important problems to ask students studying this period questions about, it is vital that you should be able to analyse the origins of the War from every angle. You will therefore need to re-read your notes on chapters 1-5 if you are to be really confident of handling this problem. Questions can be very detailed and focus on events in 1939 or they can be more general and require you to show an understanding of the whole inter-war era.

Study the following questions which are a mixture of both types of question:

1 Why did war break out over Poland in 1939?
2 'The second round of the conflict that ended in November 1918 began again in September 1939.' How much does this sum up the causes of the Second World War?
3 Why could German expansion eastwards not be prevented?
4 Why did Appeasement fail?
5 To what extent can it be argued that Hitler was planning a European War in 1939?

6 Discuss the view that French foreign policy from 1925 to 1939 was dominated by fear of Germany.
7 'The Nazi-Soviet Pact far from being a surprise was inevitable.' Discuss.
8 To what extent can the Anglo-French failure to halt Nazi aggression in the period March 1938-March 1939 be accounted for by the existence of the Rome-Berlin Axis and the Anti-Comintern Pact?

You can see from these questions that examiners can approach questions on the causes of the Second World War in a number of different ways. Arguably the most straightforward, but not necessarily the easiest approach is a direct question on why war broke out as in question 1. It is very much 'the tip of the iceberg' type of question because it is so wide ranging. Draw up a list of all the reasons why you think war broke out in September 1939. Was Poland the real cause or the 'last straw' for the western Powers? Question 2 invites you to consider the long-term causes. You should consider this explanation in light of the list of causes you have drawn up. You may come to the conclusion that far from being round two, it was in fact 'Hitler's war', or on the other hand you may come to the conclusion that it was a mixture of both. The examiner often sets questions on the relationship between Hitler's aims and Anglo-French Appeasement. In questions 3 and 4 how would you strike the balance between the weaknesses inherent in Appeasement and Hitler's responsibility for the war? Question 5 gives you the chance to explore this last aspect more fully. You should draw up a list of pros and cons which support or contradict the proposition that Hitler was contemplating a general war. You should ask yourself whether 'contemplate' means actively to plan or merely to risk war. Questions 6, 7 and 8 require a detailed knowledge of both the foreign policies of particular states and the impact of key treaties on the general international situation. To answer question 6 effectively you need to look back at chapters 4 and 5 and draw up a list of the main aims and initiatives of French foreign policy since 1925. Obviously Germany was the major preoccupation of French foreign policy, but were there at times other factors at play? For instance, how important was it for the French Government after 1936 not to pursue a foreign policy which would bitterly divide its own people? To answer question 7 you also need a considerable depth of knowledge about Russia's relations with Germany and Britain and France from the early 1920s onwards if you are to understand Stalin's thinking. You have, of course also to account for the paradox of Hitler, the great anti-Bolshevik apparently entering into partnership with Soviet Russia. Questions frequently appear on the impact of the Rome-Berlin Axis on both Italian and German policy, but usually candidates are required to follow events up to 1940 or even 1943, and therefore this topic will be discussed at the end of chapter 7.

In question 8 the examiner raises the difficult question of the impact of both the Rome-Berlin Axis and the Anti-Comintern Pact on Anglo-French policy. Here you need to explore whether these pacts really represented a realignment of the Powers. Significantly, neither Italy nor Japan declared war in September 1939, but on the other hand they were a potential combination against the Democracies and so inevitably acted as both a distraction and a threat. Can you find the evidence in chapter 6 to support this argument?

Source-based questions on *'The Outbreak of the Second World War'*

1 The Outbreak of the Sino-Japanese War

Carefully read the extracts from the French diplomat's report and Roosevelt's 'quarantine speech' on page 108. Answer the following questions:

a) To what is the French diplomat referring when he mentions 'the present tensions ... in Europe (line 1)? (3 marks)
b) Why does Roosevelt call war a 'contagion' (line1)? (2 marks)
c) Study the two documents carefully. What light do they shed on the policy of the Democracies in the Far East? (5 marks)

2 The *Hossbach Memorandum*, November 1937

Carefully read the extract on pages 109-10. Answer the following questions:

a) What was 'Germany's problem of space' (line 20)? (2 marks)
b) Why was it so important to solve this problem by 1943-5 (lines 16-20)? (3 marks)
c) As 'Contingencies 2 and 3 (lines 21-33) did not happen, does this mean that the *Hossbach Memorandum* has little value as a guide to Hitler's foreign policy? Explain your answer fully. (10 marks).

3 Appeasement and the Munich Crisis, 1938

Carefully read the extracts from Chamberlain's two statements on pages 112 and 114 and the British Ambassador's report from Tokyo on page 116. Answer the following questions:

a) What does Chamberlain's aim seem to be in November 1937? (5 marks)
b) To what extent were Britain and France to become involved in the fate of Czechoslovakia (line 3, page 114)? (5 marks)
c) How far do Chamberlain's two statements and any other evidence known to you confirm the Japanese assessment of British foreign policy during the period November-March 1937-8? (10 marks)

4 The Nazi Soviet Pact, August 1939

Look at the cartoon and the extracts from Strang's report both on page 120.

a) Why does Strang describe Soviet Russia as 'not fundamentally a friendly power'? (5 marks)
b) What point is the artist of the cartoon making about the Nazi-Soviet Pact? Is he justified? (5 marks)
c) In what ways do the cartoon and Strang's comments indicate that for Stalin an alliance with either Britain and France or Germany was bound to be a hazardous undertaking? (5 marks)

5 The Outbreak of War, 1939

Carefully read Hitler's address on 23 May to his generals on page 119, his statement of 22 August on page 121 and Halder's summary of his tactics on page 122.

a) What does Hitler mean by 'we cannot expect a repetition of Czechoslovakia' (page 119, line 3)? (2 marks)
b) On 23 May Hitler stated that 'it will be a task of dextrous diplomacy to isolate Poland' (line 8). Why did he feel that he had succeeded by 22 August? (3 marks)
c) To what extent do these documents show that Hitler fully intended to destroy Poland rather than come to a compromise over Danzig? (10 marks)

CHAPTER 7

The International Politics of the Second World War

1 Introduction

The term 'the Second World War' is a convenient but misleading description applied to the series of conflicts which convulsed the world between September 1939 and August 1945. The Second World War was not a single epic struggle, but several different wars, which in time coalesced to create a series of inter-locking conflicts on a global scale. The revisionist German historian, Ernst Nolte, has argued that Hitler in the two years between 1939 and 1941 fought three separate wars: a war to regain national territory lost in 1918-21 against Poland, then in May 1940 a war against France and Britain finally to destroy the last traces of the Versailles settlement and then a racial war against Russia in 1941, with the ultimate aim of colonising Russia in the same way that Australia and the 'Wild West' had been in the nineteenth century. Elsewhere Mussolini embarked upon his own war for empire in North Africa and the Mediterranean, while in the Far East the Sino-Japanese War, which had begun in July 1937 (see page 108) continued to escalate. Arguably the Second World War really began with the Japanese attack on Pearl Harbor and Hitler's subsequent declaration of war on America. Thereafter the 'Grand Alliance' of America, Britain and Russia inexorably bore down on the Japanese and Axis forces, but even then it waged what were essentially three different wars. Stalin was anxious to receive material and financial aid from the West, but the course of the Nazi-Soviet war was little influenced by his allies. Similarly the Pacific War remained distinct from both Stalin's war and the struggle waged by British and American forces against Hitler. The Russians did not enter the Pacific War until August 1945 while the Germans and Japanese, though allies, never co-operated militarily. Thus inevitably this mosaic of wars that came to be called collectively the Second World War ensured that beneath the Grand Alliance's rhetoric of unity there were sharply divergent aims, which were to complicate the formulation of a joint peace policy.

2 The War in Europe, 1939-41

German troops completed the occupation of Poland within six weeks and Soviet forces rapidly moved into the areas allocated to them by the Nazi-Soviet Pact. Britain and France made no effort to attack Germany in the west, and momentarily it seemed as if the brief Polish-German war might not after all lead to a general European war. Hitler, keeping his options open, offered Britain and France peace on the basis of the recreation of a small Polish state, whilst simultaneously telling his generals that his real aim was to 'smash France and to force Britain to her knees'. When both states rejected this offer on the grounds that a peace based on illegal conquests could hardly be lasting, Hitler had little option but to prepare to extend the war westwards. Inevitably he became more dependent on Soviet neutrality and supplies of raw materials to defeat the British blockade. Stalin was not slow to exploit Russia's favourable position. His policies in the winter of 1939-40 were arguably a 'dress-rehearsal' for the years immediately after 1945 when the Soviet Union was in an infinitely stronger position in eastern Europe. He persuaded Hitler to transfer Lithuania, which by the Nazi-Soviet Pact of August had originally been assigned to the German sphere of influence, to the Soviet sphere. He also rapidly negotiated pacts with the Baltic states, which reduced them to the status of satellites. When Finland refused to cede Russia a naval base and agree to the revision of her frontier, the Soviet army invaded and by February 1940 forced the Finns to comply with Stalin's demands.

In April German troops rapidly occupied both Norway and Denmark to pre-empt a clumsy British attempt to interrupt the flow of iron ore from Sweden to Germany by seizing the Norwegian ports and mining the waters around Narvik. Then on 10 May the Germans turned west and within six weeks Belgium, France and Holland were defeated and Britain was driven from the Continent. Hitler was now free to create a German Europe. Even though German policy was often hastily improvised, it does, as P.M.H. Bell has argued, reveal 'much about the nature of the war and therefore also about its origins'. In the West it was mainly a 'war about power and economic predominance'. Northern France and the Low Countries were occupied, while a satellite pro-German Vichy regime under Marshall Pétain was allowed to administer southern France. The economy of these states was ruthlessly exploited in Germany's interests and all the western European countries within the German orbit were compelled to accept trade agreements which were highly favourable to Germany. In Poland on the other hand, where a cruel, racially inspired policy was already being implemented, it had clearly become an ideological and racial war, where economics took a back seat.

The sheer scale of these victories in May 1940 at last persuaded Mussolini in June to take the plunge and belatedly to declare war on Britain and France. The defeat of France, which had seemed so strong, radically changed the balance of power on a global scale. British and American assumptions that France would be able to hold the line against Germany while they would have time to build up their armaments were now destroyed, as was Stalin's calculation that Germany and the western Powers would fatally weaken themselves in a replay of the most bloody campaigns of the First World War. In the Far East the defeat of France and the Netherlands opened up to the

Japanese tempting possibilities of taking over their colonies in Indo-China and the East Indies.

By defeating France Hitler had removed the most immediate threat to his Continental policies and his next step was to attempt to negotiate peace with Britain. On 25 June he optimistically declared:

> 1 The war in the west has ended, France has been conquered, and I shall come, in the shortest possible time, to an understanding with England. There still remains the conflict with the east. That, however, is a task which throws up world-wide problems, like the
> 5 relationship with Japan and the distribution of power in the Pacific, one might perhaps tackle it in ten years time, perhaps I shall leave it to my successor. Now we have our hands full for years to come to digest and to consolidate what we have obtained in Europe.

Yet despite this relaxed, almost statesman-like view of the future, within a year Hitler had attacked Russia. Why did he do so? Historians disagree as to whether Hitler was carrying out a long-term ideological programme or whether in H.W. Koch's words 'Hitler could only act and react within the context of the changing political constellation.' The biggest blow to Hitler's plans came when Churchill, convinced that with American aid Britain could still wage a war that would eventually wear down the German economy through 'the triad of blockade, bombing and propaganda' (D. Reynolds), refused to react to Hitler's peace feelers in June 1940. This was totally unexpected and forced Hitler to consider several options for bringing Britain to the conference table. Not only did Hitler draw up rather half-hearted plans for an invasion, but he also attempted unsuccessfully to persuade Franco and Pétain to declare war on Britain. In September 1940 pressure on Britain was intensified when a new Tripartite Pact was signed by Italy, Japan and Germany. In a key clause that was aimed at America they agreed 'to assist one another with all political, economic and military means' should one of them be attacked by a Power not yet at war in Europe or China. In November Hungary, Romania and Slovakia signed the Pact, but significantly attempts to bring in Russia failed. The Russian price for membership was too high in that Stalin demanded not only that Bulgaria should be recognised as a Russian satellite but that he should receive German backing for setting up a chain of bases in the Dardanelles and the Persian Gulf.

It is therefore possible to argue that a combination of British intransigence and mounting Russian ambitions forced Hitler to bring forward his plans for war against Russia. Weinberg argues, for instance, that the 'decision to attack the Soviet Union was Hitler's answer to the challenge of England - as it had been Napoleon's ...'. This interpretation would certainly seem to be endorsed by Hitler's assessment of the military and diplomatic situation delivered to his generals at a conference on 31 July. After stressing the difficulties involved in the invasion of the British Isles at a time when 'our small navy is only 15 per cent of [the] enemy's'. Hitler went on to argue that:

> 1 Russia is the far Eastern sword of Britain and the United States pointed at Japan... Japan, like Russia, has her programme which she wants to carry through before the end of the war ... With Russia smashed, Britain's last hope would be shattered. Germany will
> 5 then be master of Europe and the Balkans. Decision: Russia's destruction must therefore be made part of this struggle. Spring 1941. The sooner Russia is crushed, the better.

On the other hand many historians remain unconvinced that Hitler attacked Russia merely as an extension of the war against Britain. They point out that if the defeat of Britain had really been Hitler's chief priority, then he would surely have concentrated on building up sufficient naval forces and on weakening Britain in the Mediterranean. The Nazi-Soviet Pact was, of course, fragile and likely to break down when the balance of advantages favoured either of the parties sufficiently, but in June 1941 there is absolutely no evidence that Stalin was planning an imminent war against Germany. On balance it seems more likely that Hitler's long-term ideological hatred of Bolshevism and his determination to gain *lebensraum,* both of which are amply documented, played the key role in his decision to attack Russia in June 1941.

3 America, Japan and Germany, 1939-41

America held the key to eventual victory in the Second World War. If she remained neutral, it would almost certainly be impossible to dislodge the Japanese from China or to break German hegemony in Europe. However, America had a vital interest in the stability of both the Far East and Europe and with hindsight it is tempting to argue that her involvement in the European and Far Eastern wars was inevitable. But it should be remembered that, such was the strength of the isolationist lobby, Roosevelt had to proceed carefully, particularly as in the Presidential election of 1940 he had promised not to send American 'boys' to fight foreign wars. Essentially his primary aim was to keep Britain and China and then, after June 1941, Russia, fighting without having directly to involve America.

a) America and the German Threat

The fall of France was potentially a serious threat to American security as the naval bases along the northern French coast fell into German hands. If Britain accepted a compromise peace and then dropped out of the war the Germans would be in a strong position to control the Atlantic. It was therefore vital for the Americans to keep Britain fighting as the Royal Navy was their first line of defence. Thus Roosevelt defied the isolationist lobby, which wished to keep America neutral, by handing over to Britain in September 1940 some 50 aged destroyers in return for bases on Bermuda and Newfoundland. In March 1941 he persuaded Congress to pass the Lend-lease Act which permitted him to sell or lend any type of war material to any country whose defence seemed vital to the United States. This in effect meant that Britain, China and later Russia could be supplied until the end of the war with all the military equipment they needed. By the summer of 1941 the United States Navy was playing a significant role as an ally of the Royal Navy in the battle of the Atlantic. In September, for example, Roosevelt issued orders to the American Navy to shoot on sight at all German and Italian ships in the American patrol zone, which stretched right out to Greenland. By the autumn most officials in Washington were convinced that war with Germany was inevitable. To cement the unofficial Anglo-American alliance Roosevelt met Churchill on board a warship in Placentia Bay off Newfoundland and agreed on a set of common war aims, known as the Atlantic Charter, which at times echoed Woodrow Wilson's Fourteen Points of 1918 (see pages 18-20):

1 First, their countries seek no aggrandisement, territorial or other; Second, they desire to see no territorial changes that do not accord with the freely expressed wishes of the peoples concerned; Third, they respect the right of all peoples to choose the form of
5 government under which they will live ... ; Fourth, they will endeavour ... to further enjoyment by all states ... of access, on equal terms, to the trade and to the raw materials of the world which are needed for their economic prosperity; ... Eighth, they believe that all of the nations of the world, for realistic as well as
10 spiritual reasons must come to the abandonment of force ... they believe, pending establishment of a wider and permanent system of general security, that the disarmament of such nations is essential.

b) The Road to Pearl Harbor

It is tempting to argue that the Japanese attack on Pearl Harbor on 7 December was inevitable. One historian (J.G. Utley) has stressed that 'the Japanese-American conflict grew out of two mutually exclusive views of world order'. Japan, regarding herself as a 'have-not' power, attempted to guarantee her access to markets and raw materials by gradually dominating economically and politically not only China but the whole of south-east Asia. To the Americans, as was made clear in the Atlantic Charter, it was an article of both faith and practical economics that they should be able to trade and invest freely in China and elsewhere. With Germany having established a self-sufficient siege economy in Europe, it became even more imperative from the American point of view to stop Japan from doing the same in Asia. Washington responded to each fresh extension of Japanese power not only by building up its naval forces in the Pacific, but by restricting more and more tightly the exports of potential war materials to Japan, a measure which in fact only intensified the Japanese drive for economic self-sufficiency. Both sides seemed therefore to be on a collision course. But history is never that simple. There were sufficiently ambiguous and conflicting signals coming out of Tokyo to encourage Roosevelt and the American State Department sometimes to believe that if sufficient economic pressure were applied, Japan would be forced to pull out of China and the influence of the army would be discredited in Tokyo.

In June 1940 Hitler's victories strengthened the hand of the hawks in Tokyo who advocated the occupation of the European colonies in south-east Asia. A relatively moderate government, which wished to avoid confrontation with America, was replaced by a more anti-western regime under Konoe, which openly proclaimed its aim of creating a Japanese-dominated Asia. Washington responded by suspending exports of vital aviation fuel and lubricating oil. To neutralise growing American opposition the Japanese then tried to negotiate a Four-Power pact with the Axis states and Russia. They succeeded in reaching an agreement with Germany and Italy in September and they signed a five year treaty of neutrality with Stalin the following spring. But the German invasion of the Soviet Union in June 1941 terminated any prospect of a grand four Power alliance against Britain and America. Konoe indeed then urged that Japan should desert the Axis Powers and come to an agreement with Britain and America, but he was over-ruled by his foreign minister and the armed services, who all believed that Hitler would quickly defeat the Russians. Thus Tokyo and Washington remained on a collision course. In July the Japanese occupied the southern half of the French Indo-China and the Americans responded by imposing a comprehensive oil embargo on Japan. The oil embargo confronted the Japanese with the alternative of either seeing their war machine paralysed through lack of oil or of launching within a few months at the latest a pre-emptive strike against their enemies. In early December they received verbal assurances from Ribbentrop that, in the event of a Japanese attack, Germany would also declare war against America even though strictly speaking the Tripartite Pact did not commit Germany to such an action as it was a defensive alliance only. Thus at dawn on 7 December the Japanese felt sufficiently confident to launch their attack on the American base at Pearl Harbor.

Hitler's declaration of war on the United States on 9 December can in retrospect be seen as a major error as one cannot with certainty say that Roosevelt, confronted with war in the Far East, would have been able to persuade Congress to declare war on Germany as well. However, it could be argued that informally the Americans were already at war with Germany and that Hitler's declaration of war was therefore both a recognition of reality and a politically calculated gesture of solidarity aimed at encouraging the Japanese to tie down the Americans in the Pacific so that they could not assist the British in the Atlantic.

4 The Grand Alliance

In military terms the Grand Alliance of Great Britain, Soviet Russia and the United States of America was one of the most successful alliances in history. By August 1945 it had totally defeated its enemies. Nevertheless, its members had divergent and at times contradictory policies and aims. Initially the most divisive issue in the alliance was the question of opening up a second front against Germany. The Russians were so suspicious of Anglo-American procrastination in 1943 that they temporarily withdrew their ambassadors from London and Washington and put out exploratory peace feelers to Hitler, who rashly rejected them, believing that victory was still possible. There were also tensions between the British and the Americans, who were suspicious of Churchill's imperialism and suspected that his interest in military operations in the Mediterranean was really a ploy to safeguard British imperial interests there.

By 1943, when the tide was strongly turning against Japan and the Axis Powers, the future shape of the post-war world began increasingly to preoccupy the leaders of the Grand Alliance. The most complex problems were concerned with the future of eastern Europe and Germany and the creation of a new global security system to replace the League of Nations.

a) Eastern Europe and the Balkans

Of all the problems facing the Allies the future of eastern Europe and the Balkans was the most divisive. In theory the Allies had the chance to re-draw the political map of the whole region, but in reality by 1945 it was clear that the real arbiter of eastern Europe was Soviet Russia. The British initially, as an insurance against a future German revival, proposed a series of federations consisting of a Scandinavian grouping in the north, a central European bloc made up of Czechoslovakia, Poland, Romania and Bulgaria and an Austrian-Hungarian-Yugoslav Federation in the south, but this was opposed by both Russia and America. To Roosevelt it seemed a reversion to old-fashioned power politics. At most he was ready to see the creation of an independent Croatia under the protection of the United Nations. Stalin was not bothered about the rights and wrongs of power politics. He was quite ready to concede to the British, who wanted to protect their interests in the eastern Mediterranean, the predominant interest in Greece but he did not want to see Poland put into a federation strong enough to be independent of Soviet Russia. Of the Allied leaders Stalin had the most detailed demands. He wanted the restoration of all the territory Soviet Russia had held on the eve of the German invasion of June 1941: the Baltic states, the eastern areas of Finland, Bukovina and Besserabia in Romania, and particularly the Polish territory allotted to Russia by the Nazi-soviet Pact. Anxious to keep the Grand Alliance intact Churchill and Roosevelt conceded at the Teheran Conference in November 1943 Stalin's demands for eastern Poland. Gradually in 1944 it became clearer that Stalin was also going to insist on the installation of a pro-soviet government in Warsaw and veto the restoration of the Polish government in exile in London, which had been set up in 1940. Essentially Stalin was determined to protect Soviet Russia by creating a ring of satellite states. As it was the Red Army which drove the Germans out of eastern Europe, it was his philosophy rather than that of the Atlantic Charter that was to be decisive there.

b) The Future of Germany

The Anglo-American and Russian plans for the future of Germany made the Treaty of Versailles seem mild in comparison. All three Allies agreed that after her defeat Germany should be initially occupied by Allied troops and then partitioned into three or even five different states. At the Quebec Conference in September 1944 Roosevelt proposed a plan devised by Morgenthau, the Secretary of the American Treasury, which as a

> programme for eliminating the war-making industries in the Ruhr and in the Saar is looking forward to converting Germany into a country primarily agricultural and pastoral in character.

Churchill accepted, perhaps, as one historian has argued, because it was the price he had to pay for the extension of Lend-Lease aid until the end of the Japanese war. The plan was almost immediately subjected to searching criticism by both British and American officials who, in arguments that were reminiscent of those in Maynard Keynes's *The Economic Consequences of the Peace* (see page 49), pointed out its negative implications for both the future payment of reparations by the Germans and the financial stability of Europe. By 1945 the Morgenthau Plan was quietly dropped.

c) The Replacement of the League of Nations

As with President Wilson, his predecessor at the end of the First World

War, the creation of a world security organisation rapidly became the key to Roosevelt's plans for rebuilding the post-war world. But, unlike Wilson, he was very careful to keep in step with public opinion at home and to ensure support from the Republicans who in 1920 had stopped America from joining the League of Nations. In August 1944 the constitution of the future United Nations was discussed at Dumbarton Oaks, near Washington. What emerged was essentially an American blueprint for a new world order. The basic organisation of the United Nations was similar to the League's in that it consisted of the Security Council on which the four Great Powers, Britain, China the USA and USSR all had permanent seats, a General Assembly where representatives of the other states sat, an International Court of Justice and an International Secretariat. Unlike the Council of the League of Nations it was initially envisaged by the Americans that the Security Council would be responsible for peace and security on a global scale and would be able to insist on the other member states carrying out its decisions. These would be taken by majority voting. However, Stalin, who was anxious to ensure that Russia would not be regularly outvoted, insisted on the right of each permanent member of the Security Council to have a veto on the implementation of policies it disliked. In essence this was conceded at the Yalta Conference and confirmed when the United Nations was set up at the San Francisco Conference in April 1945. This proviso was significantly to limit the future power of the United Nations.

5 The Yalta and Potsdam Conferences, February and July 1945

In February 1945 the details of the post-war settlement were finalised by the three Allied leaders at Yalta. Apart from agreeing to set up the United Nations, key decisions were taken on the frontiers of Poland and the temporary division of Germany into Allied zones of occupation as well as on Russia's eventual declaration of war against Japan. As a consequence of the Cold War the Yalta Conference has become in retrospect almost as controversial as the Peace Conference of 1919. Subsequently both American Republicans and European Conservatives have bitterly criticised Roosevelt for allowing himself allegedly to have been hopelessly outwitted by Stalin and thus led into abandoning eastern Europe to Russian control. Today most historians would argue that this interpretation is flawed. Yalta was only the second summit conference attended by all three leaders of the Grand Alliance. Each had his own priorities and aims. Roosevelt under pressure from public opinion at home wanted to persuade Russia to declare war on Japan and, as a member of the Security Council of the United Nations, to become one of the pillars of the new world order. On the other hand, Stalin was intent on gaining the maximum security against any future invasion from Germany. Churchill was concerned to secure a zone of occupation in Germany for liberated France, as she was Britain's main European ally and would be needed in the future to help maintain the balance of power against Soviet Russia. He also wanted an independent democratic Poland as Britain had, after all, gone to war to preserve Polish independence.

In the hard bargaining at the Conference reasonable compromises appeared to be struck. France secured an occupation zone and Stalin agreed to declare war on Japan two or three months after the hostilities with Germany had finished, provided Russia was given the Kuril Islands, southern Sakhalin and the lease of Port Arthur from China. He even seemed to concede free Polish elections, although he refused to abandon the pro -Soviet government in Warsaw. There was agreement that Russia should keep the Polish territory she had gained in September 1939, and that Poland's western frontiers should be fixed when the peace conference met. Western fears about the future of eastern Europe were initially allayed by the Declaration on Liberated Europe which unambiguously stated:

> 1 The establishment of order in Europe and the rebuilding of national economic life must be achieved by processes which will

Destiny's child, The Chicago Tribune, *1945*

enable the liberated peoples to destroy the last vestiges of Nazism and Fascism and to create democratic institutions of their own
5 choice.

In practice such a rousing declaration was bound to be ambiguous. By the summer of 1945 eastern Europe was not, as in 1919, a power vacuum to be filled by small independent states. Soviet troops were in full occupation and there was no way that Stalin would tolerate any but friendly pro-Communist regimes there. Britain and America similarly were unwilling to tolerate a Russian presence in Italy, Greece or the eastern Mediterranean.

The leaders of the Grand alliance met at Potsdam in July 1945. It was to be the last Great Power summit for ten years. After bitter disagreements which nearly terminated the conference Britain and America gave provisional agreement to the extension of Poland's western frontiers to the Oder-Neisse line (a border following the course of the rivers Oder and Neisse) and a scheme whereby each occupying Power would extract reparations from its own zone, although Russia would also be allotted some 25 per cent of the total equipment available in the Ruhr. The increasing division of Europe into two blocs was emphasised when Russian demands for the internationalisation of the Ruhr and a mandate over the ex-Italian colony of Libya were rejected, while western requests for a greater say in the Soviet dominated eastern and south-eastern Europe were similarly vetoed by Stalin.

The same distrust was evident in the weeks preceding the Russian declaration of war on Japan. As soon as the atom bomb had been tested successfully, the Americans became markedly less keen on Russia entering the Pacific war. When the bomb was dropped on Hiroshima on 6 August, the Russians, alarmed that they might be cheated out of what had been promised to them at Yalta, declared war against Japan two days later. After the Japanese surrender of 15 August, Stalin received the territorial rewards that had been promised him at Yalta, but the Americans effectively excluded Russia from participating in the occupation of Japan.

6 The Peace Treaties

Because the three leaders were aware of the muddled way in which the Paris Peace Conference of 1919 had been conducted, it was agreed at Potsdam that a Council of Foreign Minister should be set up to prepare peace treaties with the five German satellite powers - Italy, Romania, Bulgaria, Hungary and Finland. A Preliminary Peace Conference met in Paris in 1946 and in February 1947 the five peace treaties were signed. Compared to the great upheavals of 1919-20 only minor frontier adjustments were made. Disagreements about the value of former German property that Austria was to hand over to the Soviet government delayed the Austrian Peace Treaty until 1955. Similarly Russo-American disagreements about conference procedure delayed a Japanese settlement until in 1951 a treaty, which Russia and the new Communist China refused to recognise, was signed between Japan, America and the Western Powers. At Potsdam the three Great Powers, dropping their insistence on partition, had agreed to sign a peace treaty with Germany, once a unified independent Germany had been restored. In 1945 few foresaw that, as a consequence of the Cold War, Germany would remain divided between the Eastern and Western bloc until 1990.

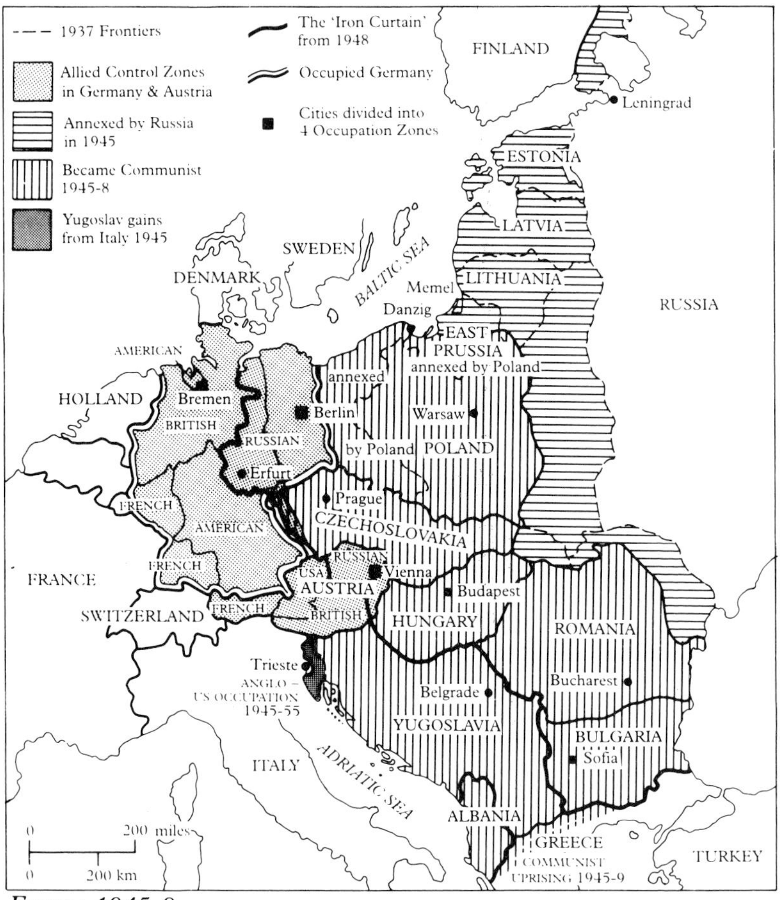

Europe 1945-8

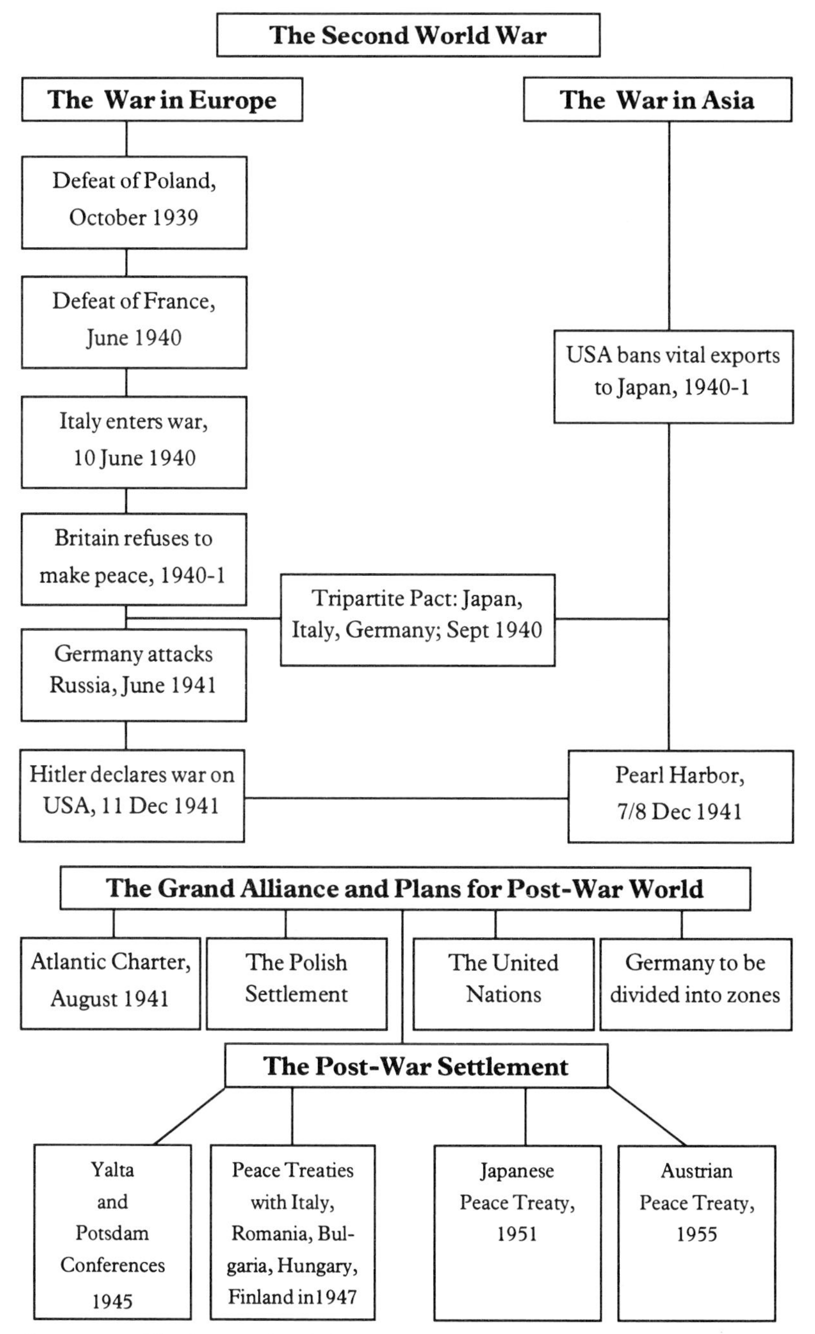

Summary - The International Politics of the Second World War

Making notes on *'The International Politics of the Second World War'*

This chapter has three main themes aiming: (i) to show how separate wars in Europe, the Middle East and the Far East became linked together in a global war; (ii) to analyse the reasons why Hitler attacked Soviet Russia in June 1941; (iii) to explore the uneasy alliance between the partners of the Grand Alliance.

When making your notes on this chapter, you should concentrate on the following topics:

1 Hitler's policy from September 1939-June 1941. Was the conquest of most of western Europe just a preliminary to a move eastwards to gain *Lebensraum* or was Hitler forced into attacking Russia by Britain's refusal to surrender?
2 American policy towards Germany and Japan, September 1939-December 1941. Was America an ally of Britain in all but name?
3 What were the issues that most divided the members of the Grand Alliance? Was it only the need for a common front against Germany that kept it together?

Answering essay questions on *'The International Politics of the Second World War'*

As the development of German war aims during the Second World War provides many clues to understanding Hitler's pre-war foreign policy, examiners often set questions which expect you to link events in the 1930s with the war years. Study the following questions which are restricted to the period 1930-45:

1 Why did Hitler sign a non-aggression pact with Stalin in August 1939 only to attack Soviet Russia in 1941?
2 What were the consequences of the Axis pact for Italian and German foreign policy up to 1940?
3 Was there anything inevitable about America's entry into the war in December 1941?
4 How seriously was the effectiveness of the Grand Alliance threatened by inter-Allied disputes, 1941-5?

Question 1 targets one of the key problems you have to consider when studying Hitler's foreign policy: did Hitler mean what he said in *Mein Kampf* about the need to acquire *lebensraum* at Russia's expense, or was this just a fantasy, as A.J.P. Taylor would have us believe? If, as most historians do, you take Hitler's expressed aims seriously, then the Nazi-Soviet Pact and the defeat of France were surely just preliminaries to an attack on Russia. On the other hand is it arguable that his failure to defeat Britain forced him into a premature attack on Russia? Question 2 concentrates on the international consequences of the Axis Pact. You should look back at your notes of chapters 5 and 6 and then draw up lists of how you think the Pact influenced the policy of both countries. Could it be argued that its main importance was political rather than military? It frightened the Democracies and made them less willing to stand up to Hitler in 1938. Is it thereafter of only marginal importance to the course of events? Question 3 is a deceptively simple question, which you will need to think about quite a lot before answering. For instance, which war was implied - the Far Eastern or European? The examiner will also expect you to trace American policy towards Japan and Germany and to explain why it was Hitler who declared war on America. Question 4 also appears to be straightforward, but needs a lot of preliminary thought on your part. Is 'effectiveness' to be used purely in the military sense or can it be applied to the diplomatic task of preparing the peace?

Source-based questions on *'The International Politics of the Second World War'*

1 The Nazi Invasion of Russia, June 1941

Carefully read the extracts from Hitler's statements of 25 June and 31 July 1941 on pages 131 and 132.

a) Why did Hitler think that he would be able to come to an understanding with Britain (line 2, page 131)? Why was he unable to do so? (5 marks)
b) What did Hitler mean by 'Russia is the Far Eastern sword of Britain and the United States' (line 1 page 132)? (3 marks)
c) What light do these extracts shed on Hitler's intentions towards Russia in the summer of 1940? (7 marks)

2 Planning the Peace, 1941-5

Carefully read the extracts from the *Atlantic Charter* on page 133, the Morgenthau Plan on page 136, the *Declaration on Liberated Europe,* pages 138-9 and look at the cartoon on page 138.

a) Explain the meaning of the fourth point of the *Atlantic Charter* (lines 5-8). To what extent might this remove a major source of global conflict? (5 marks)
b) To what extent does the Morgenthau Plan contradict the *Declaration on Liberated Europe* and the Atlantic Charter? (5 marks)
c) Study the cartoon carefully. Explain fully the point the artist is making. (5 marks)

CHAPTER 8

Conclusion: Change and Continuity

How should the period 1914-45 be assessed? Was it a period of the German Wars or a new Thirty Years War of which the German wars were only a part? Or was it a European civil war? However much historians may debate about this period, there is no doubt that 1945 or perhaps even 1941, marked the end of European global hegemony. The European Great Powers were eclipsed by America and Soviet Russia.

As early as 1919 this hegemony had been challenged when America emerged from the First World War as the dominant world financial Power. At this stage, however, the USA still lacked the will to play the role of a Great Power. In the words of one historian (Kathleen Burke) 'the US took a look at the centre court of international politics and refused to play'. In 1919 France had been in a paradoxical position. As a consequence of Germany's defeat and America's return to isolation she had become by default the world's greatest military Power, but it was a not a role that she could sustain. In 1945 France was a defeated country, only temporarily restored to the ranks of the Great Powers by a Britain desperate to have an ally in western Europe. In 1919 Russia, like Germany, had been a defeated Power. The peace treaties had, in effect, been imposed on her as they were on Germany, Austria, Hungary, Bulgaria and Turkey. She had not been consulted about the borders of Turkey or of Poland. After the Bolshevik victory in the civil war the Soviet Union's greatest priority was to defend the revolution and modernise the economy. So well was this achieved that, despite the weakening of the Red Army through the purges of the late 1930s, unexpectedly she was able ultimately to defeat Hitler. The political vacuum that this created in eastern Europe enabled her to regain all the territory she had lost since the Crimean War of 1854-6. In 1945 therefore, despite defeat and revolution in 1917 and the subsequent civil war, she had re-emerged as a Great Power. How much was this due to Hitler who in 1941 appeared to 'snatch defeat from the jaws of victory' by not only attacking Russia in June but in December also declaring war on America?

At first glance the position of Britain had remained unchanged. In both wars she had played a pivotal role. In 1919 with the defeat of Germany and, as an added bonus, the weakening of her old imperial rival Russia, she had emerged a clear winner, but by 1941 Britain was bankrupt and the least important member of the Grand Alliance. Like France in 1919 she had all the trappings of a Great Power, but it was a status that she could not sustain. No wonder modern historians sometimes raise the question whether Britain's mistake was to have gone to war against Nazi Germany, but did Britain in reality have any other option if she wished to retain her status as a Great Power? The other Power to gain decisively at Versailles had been Japan. She had increased her power effortlessly in China and in the Pacific at Germany's expense, and had also been given a permanent seat on the Council of the League of Nations. However, she was not able to maximise her strength in the Far East until Germany and Italy upset the balance of power in Europe after 1936.

At the end of the First World War European prosperity could not be rebuilt until America partially re-emerged from isolation to assist in restoring European finances after the French occupation of the Ruhr had triggered hyper-inflation in Germany and also seriously weakened the franc. The brief stabilisation of the European economy that occurred between 1924 and 1929 had some similarities with the stabilisation of the western European economy after 1948. In 1924 a fragile economic and diplomatic equilibrium was created as a consequence of the Dawes Plan and the British Locarno guarantee. As in 1948 American money did flow into Germany and help revive the economy. Confidence was further strengthened by a growing trust between France and Germany symbolised by the Briand-Stresemann relationship and the increasing talk about a European union, which to some extent anticipated the debates of the 1950s. Are historians correct to see the 1920s as a 'darkening twilight of the liberal era'? One American scholar, Charles S. Maier points out that it was in fact a period of new ideas for economic and political co-operation, which could have provided an escape from Great Power conflict. Indeed he argues that if it was a 'twilight decade, the 1920s was one of morning as well as dusk'. The crucial difference, however, between the two post-war periods is that in the 1920s the financing of the European economy was left to private investors, mainly American, while in the late-1940s, through Marshall Aid, finance was guaranteed by the American state itself and was therefore more secure.

Nevertheless, even Marshall Aid might have faltered in the face of a recession on the scale of the Great Depression of 1929-30. Most historians agree that the Depression was a pre-condition for the rise of Hitler and the success of Japanese militarism in the Far East and thus a major cause of the Second World War. On the other hand if you believe that there was a continuity in German foreign policy and that the Second World War was merely a renewal of Germany's attempt to dominate Europe, would you downgrade the importance of the Depression?

The Depression was instrumental in pushing America back into isolation just when Europe most needed her. German and Japanese expansion in the 1930s were facilitated by American inactivity in the Far East and the failure of the Anglo-French policy of appeasement in Europe. Only in March 1939 when Hitler occupied Bohemia and Britain guaranteed Poland did it become quite clear, as it also had been in 1917-18, that Britain could not tolerate unlimited German expansion in eastern Europe. The last chance of deterring Hitler was destroyed when Stalin decided to sign a neutrality pact with Hitler rather than a military alliance with Britain and France in order to regain some of Russia's former Polish territory. How inevitable were the events that led to war in 1938-9? What role did miscalculation or just bad luck play in their unfolding? If you are convinced that Hitler was determined on war, then you will clearly be very sceptical of Taylor's argument that there was nothing inevitable about the outbreak of the European war in September 1939. On the other hand, would a crucial difference have been made if Britain and France could have kept Italy on their side or negotiated a successful alliance with Soviet Russia? Is there any truth in the argument that the British feared Stalin more than they did Hitler?

The Second World War was a very different war from the First World War in that it consisted of several distinct wars that only gradually merged into one great war. Thanks to the Nazi-Soviet pact, Hitler unlike Bethmann Hollweg in 1914, could afford to risk a minor war (against Poland) escalating into a major war against Britain and France because he no longer faced the danger of a protracted struggle on two fronts. The defeat of France encouraged Japanese expansion in the Far East, but it was essentially the growing threat to America's position in the Atlantic that enabled Roosevelt to modify the Neutrality Acts and to keep Britain in the war. It is arguable that the ever more serious clashes between the American navy and German U-boats would in time have brought America into the war, but it was the massive miscalculation of the Japanese at Pearl Harbor and Hitler's declaration of war on America that finally brought about this crucial event. This, combined with Hitler's attack on Russia in June 1941, made the defeat of the Axis Powers inevitable, as long as the Allies held together, and this unity was not a foregone conclusion. By 1943 at the latest, America felt sufficiently self-confident to develop and begin to enforce her own ideas for the post-war world by making use of her massive military and financial power.

The years 1941-50 witnessed a major diplomatic revolution. Not only were the Japanese and the Axis Powers defeated and their territory occupied, but for the western nations the old German danger was replaced until 1989 by the Soviet threat. This had briefly been a disturbing possibility in 1919-20, but now with the Red Army on the Elbe, it had become a very real danger. Consequently the old anti-German grouping of Britain, Russia and France, first formed in 1904-7 was replaced after 1949 by a new anti-Soviet alliance, led by America, and composed of Italy, Japan (which in October 1951 signed a security agreement with Washington allowing the establishment of American bases on its territory), Western Germany, Britain and France. Both America and Russia had become 'super' Powers with formidable nuclear arsenals. Paradoxically this 'cold war' following on the heels of the 'hot' war helped produce a settlement in Europe which was more stable than that negotiated at Versailles in 1919. In eastern Europe the

Soviet Union acted as 'a durable enforcing agent'(Stevenson). Together with its allies it annexed about a quarter of Germany's pre-war territory and set up a satellite state, the German Democratic Republic, in its former zone of occupation. There was thus no question of any independent renewal of hostilities by Germany and the German 'bogey' became a thing of the past. To counter the threat of Communism to western Europe, British and American troops were stationed in western Germany permanently and America used her overwhelming financial strength to revive the western European economies. Thanks to the Marshall Plan the Americans assisted the West German economy by promoting a general western European recovery. The French demands of 1944-6 for a second harsh peace with Germany were thus gradually forgotten and the way was opened up for a Franco-German economic rapprochement, which was realised through the subsequent formation of the Coal and Steel Community and the European Economic Community. An economic partnership between France and Germany had been an option which the more far-sighted French and German politicians had considered back in the early 1920s, but arguably it was only an option that could work once Germany had been decisively weakened.

Working on the *Conclusion*

There is no need to make any detailed notes on this chapter, but it is important to consider what key themes keep repeating themselves in chapters 1-7 of this book and why they do so. You need to make up your mind about two main groups of questions:

1 The role of Germany, 1914-45. Is this the central issue of the period?
2 Are therefore all the other issues such as Italian and Japanese imperialism, the emergence of America as a Great Power, British and French decline, the impact of the Depression, the role of Soviet Russia and the attempts to create a system of collective security, essentially only of secondary importance and to be analysed in relation to Germany?

To answer these questions you must decide on your criteria. How do you define a 'central issue'? Is it one that ultimately dominates all other issues, so that they seem both to contemporaries and historians to be of subordinate importance to the central theme? If in time these 'side issues' do become in themselves dominant, is it only because the central problem has been 'solved'? For example, the clash between Communism and the West dominated the world after 1945. Was this only so since the German issue had apparently been solved by the defeat of Hitler?

Once you have decided on your criteria, you will need to look back at your notes of the preceding chapters and follow developments of the various issues listed above. Whatever you decide about the role Germany played in this period you will need to analyse the attempts by the European Powers and America to contain her through wars, treaties, appeasement and European integration during the period 1914-45. Whilst doing this, you may then well come to the conclusion that the German problem only dominated because, for example, the Russian Revolution temporarily upset the European balance of power or that it was only a consequence of the Great Depression. Whatever your conclusions, you will need to have an overall grasp of the period covered by this book and opinions of your own on the historical debates which many aspects of these troubled years have given rise to. You should then be able to face the examiner with confidence!

Chronological Table

1914	28 June, Franz Ferdinand assassinated
	28 July, Austria declared war on Serbia
	1 August, Germany declared war on Russia
	3 August, Germany declared war on France
	4 August, Great Britain declared war on Germany
	23 August, Japan declared war on Germany
	12 October, Turkey joined Central Powers
1915	26 April, Treaty of London signed by Italy, France, Britain and Russia
	23 May, Italy declared war on Austria-Hungary
1916	9 May, Sykes-Picot agreement on British and French spheres of influence in the Middle East
1917	31 January, Germans started unrestricted submarine warfare
	12 March, first Russian Revolution
	6 April, America declared war on Germany
	7 November, second Russian or Bolshevik Revolution
1918	8 January, Wilson announced 14 Points
	3 March, Treaty of Brest-Litovsk signed
	11 November, The German Armistice
1919	18 January, Peace Conference opened at Paris
	30 June, Treaty of Versailles signed with Germany
	10 September, Treaty of St. Germain signed with Austria
	27 November, Treaty of Neuilly signed with Bulgaria
1920	4 June, Treaty of Trianon signed with Hungary
	10 August, Treaty of Sèvres signed with Turkey
1921	April, Reparation Commission fixed German debt at 132 billion gold marks
1922	April, Genoa conference and Treaty of Rapallo signed between Germany and Soviet Russia
	23 September-1 October, Chanak Incident
1923	11 January, French and Belgian troops occupied the Ruhr
	July, Treaty of Sevres finally revised at Lausanne Conference
1924	April, Dawes Commission published its recommendations
1925	5-16 October, Locarno Conference
1926	January, Allies evacuated Cologne Zone
	September, Germany joined League of Nations
1928	27 August, Kellogg-Briand pact signed by 15 states
1929	August, Hague Conference: Young Plan and Allied Evacuation of Rhineland approved
	29 October, Wall Street Crash
1931	March, German proposal for customs union with Austria
1932	February, Disarmament Conference met at Geneva
	July, Lausanne conference: Reparations virtually abolished
	September, Mukden incident
1933	30 January, Hitler appointed Chancellor of Germany
	February, Japan left League of Nations
	October, Germany left both League and Disarmarment Conference

1934 January, German-Polish non-Aggression Pact
July, Nazi uprising in Austria failed

1935 January, Saar plebiscite
March, Hitler reintroduced conscription
April, Stresa Front
May, Franco-Soviet Pact
June, Anglo-German Naval Agreement
October, Abyssinia invaded by Italy

1936 March, Rhineland reoccupied by Germany
July, Spanish Civil War began
October/November, Rome-Berlin Axis. German-Japanese Anti-Commintern Pact

1937 July, Japan attacked China

1938 12 March, German occupation of Austria
20-22 May, Rumours that Germany was about to invade Czechoslovakia
8 September, Sudeten Germans broke off negotiations with Prague
15 September, Chamberlain visited Hitler at Berchtesgaden
22-23 September, Chamberlain at Bad Godesberg
28 September, Hitler accepted Mussolini's plan for Four-Power talks
29-30 Four-Power Conference at Munich

1939 15 March, Germany occupied Bohemia and Moravia
21 March, German-Polish talks on Danzig
23 March, Lithuania handed over Memel to Germany
31 March, Provisional Anglo-French guarantee of Poland
7 April, Italian occupation of Albania
13 April, Anglo-French guarantee of Greece and Romania
14 April, Anglo-French negotiations with Soviet Union start
28 April, Hitler terminated Anglo-German Naval Agreement and German-Polish Pact
22 May, Pact of Steel signed in Berlin
23 August Nazi-Soviet Pact
1 September, Germany invaded Poland
3 September, Britain and France declared war on Germany

1940 10 June, Italy declared war on Britain and France
22 June, Franco-German Armistice
27 September, Tripartite Pact signed by Germany, Italy and Japan

1941 22 June, German invasion of Russia
7/8 December, Japanese attack Pearl Harbor. America declared war on Japan
11 December, Germany declared war on the United States

1943 November-December, Churchill, Roosevelt and Stalin met at Teheran

1944 August, Dumbarton Oaks Conference on setting up United Nations

1945 February, Yalta Conference
9 May, Unconditional surrender of Germany
26 June, United Nations Charter signed at San Francisco July-August, Potsdam Conference
6 August, Atom bomb dropped on Hiroshima
8 August, Russia declared war on Japan
15 August, Unconditional surrender of Japan

Further Reading

There are thousands of books on this period in many different languages. If you are looking for a good introductory survey, you will find the following studies very helpful:

M. Kitchen, *Europe between the Wars,* Longman, 1988
R. Parker, *Europe, 1919-45,* Weidenfeld and Nicolson, 1969
E. Wiskemann, *Europe of the Dictators, 1919-1945,* Fontana, 1966

The international politics of the First World War is a complicated topic, but it is dealt with in a skilful and above all readable way in chapter XXIII of

A.J.P. Taylor, *The Struggle for Mastery in Europe, 1848-1918,* (paperback edition), Oxford University Press, 1971

A very useful but more specialised study on both the First World War and the peace conferences of 1919-20, is

D. Stevenson, *The First World War and International Politics,* Oxford University Press (paperback), 1991

If you are interested in finding out more about the peace settlements

G. Schulz, *Revolutions and Peace Treaties, 1917-20* is a helpul survey of all the treaties. Above all it does not neglect the Russian and German dimensions. For the Paris Peace Conference of 1919, a detailed but absorbing book is

A.J. Mayer, *Politics and Diplomacy in Peacemaking: Containment and Counter-Revolution at Versailles,* Weidenfeld and Nicolson, 1968

The majority of historical studies on the international politics of this period focus on the coming of the Second World War, but there is a good analysis of Anglo-French-German relations, 1921-39 in chapter 3 (pages 50-59) of

J. Hiden, *Germany and Europe, 1919-39,* Longman, 1977 (2nd. edition, 1993)

A more specialised study of the Locarno era is

J. Jacobson, *Locarno Diplomacy. Germany and the West, 1925-29,* Princeton, 1972

A detailed but readable history of the League of Nations is

F.S. Northedge, *The League of Nations, its Life and Times,* Leicester University Press, 1986

A much shorter but more difficult history of the League can be found in *The New Cambridge Modern History,* Vol XII, chapter IX, Cambridge University Press, (second edition) 1968

There are an enormous number of books on the 1930s and the immediate causes of the Second World War. You should certainly read **A.J.P. Taylor,** *The Origins of the Second World War,* Hamish Hamilton, 1961

But you will need to compare Taylor's views with those of other historians. The following are excellent studies which will help you to make up your own mind about Taylor's arguments:

C. Thorne, *The Approach to War,* Macmillan, 1967
P.M.H. Bell, *The Second World War in Europe,* Longman 1986
R. Overy, *The Origins of the Second World War,* Longman, 1987

A good introduction to the historical controversy on the causes of the Second World War is in two collection of essays

The Origins of the Second World War, **ed E.M. Robertson,** Macmillan, 1971 and *Paths to War. New essays on the Origins of the Second World War,* **ed. R. Boyce and E. M. Robertson,** Macmillan, 1989

The most informative book on the international politics of the Second World War, which covers the whole period from September 1939 up to the Austrian Treaty of May 1955 is

J. Wheeler-Bennett and A. Nicholls. *The Semblance of Peace. The Political Settlement after the Second World War,* Macmillan, 1972

A highly readable study of the Second World War which deals with both the military and the political dimension of the conflict is

M. Kitchen, *A World in Flames. A Short History of the Second World War in Europe, 1939-45,* Longman 1990

If you want to look more closely at Hitler's foreign policy. there are a large number of books to choose from. A concise analysis can be found in

W. Carr, *Arms, Autarky and Aggression. A Study in German Foreign Policy, 1933-39,* Edward Arnold, (reprinted) 1979, **D.G. Williamson,** *The Third Reich,* chapters 9-11, Longman, 1982

A much more detailed study is

G.L. Weinberg, *The Foreign Policy of Hitler's Germany;* vol i Diplomatic Revolution, 1933-36; vol ii Starting World War II. 1937-39, University of Chicago Press, 1970 and 1980

A detailed study of Italian foreign policy over this period is

C.J. Lowe and F. Mazari, *Italian Foreign Policy, 1870-1940,* Routledge, 1975

French foreign policy is well dealt with in

J. Néré, *The Foreign Policy of France from 1914 to 1945,* Routledge, 1975

If you need to look more carefully at French policy on the eve of the Second World War an excellent and readable study is

A. Adamthwaite, *France and the Coming of the Second World War, 1936-9,* Cass, 1977

For more about the international impact of the Spanish Civil War, the classic account is still in

Book Three of **H. Thomas,** *The Spanish Civil War,* Penguin, 1965

A much shorter account is in chapter 4 of **H. Browne,** *Spain's Civil War,* Longman, 1983

The best short analysis of Soviet Foreign policy is still in

G.F. Kennan, *Soviet Foreign Policy, 1917-1941,* Greenwood Press, reprinted, 1978

For American foreign policy the best survey is in

A. Decondes, *A History of American Foreign Policy,* vol ii, Charles Scribner's sons, New York, 3rd. edition, 1978

There is an excellent selection of documents covering all aspects of the build up to the Second World War in:

A.P. Adamthwaite, *The Making of the Second World War,* Allen and Unwin, 1979

There are also useful collections of documents in the books mentioned above by Kennan, Lowe and Mazari, Néré, Overy and Williamson.

Index